Think Like A Giraffe

A Reach For The Sky Guide
In Creativity And Maximum Performance

Also By Stephen M. Gower, CSP

The Art Of Killing Kudzu
Management By Encouragement

Celebrate The Butterflies
Presenting With Confidence In Public

What Do They See When They See You Coming?
The Power Of Perception Over Reality

Upsize Selling
Increase Your Sales With The Mix Of Six

Like A Pelican In The Desert
Leadership Redefined: Beyond Awkwardness

Have You Encouraged Someone Today?
366 Ways To Practice Encouragement

The Focus Crisis
Nurturing Focus Within A Culture Of Change

Think Like A Giraffe

A Reach For The Sky Guide
In Creativity And Maximum Performance

Stephen M. Gower, CSP

Lectern Publishing
P. O. Box 1065, Toccoa, GA 30577

First edition, published 1997 by LECTERN PUBLISHING, P. O. Box 1065, Toccoa, GA 30577.
Second Printing, 1998.

Library of Congress Catalog Card Number. 96-80507

ISBN 1-880150-96-4

Dedication

To Holly Peeples – first as my student, then as a vital part of preparing my manuscripts for publishing, Holly has always deserved an A.

Acknowledgement

My "where I have been" has everything in the world to do with what I now write. What I now write is an extension of the absorption of experiences, ideas, and relationships that have gifted me for more than half of a century.

My mother continues to remind me that there are very few original thoughts these days. She is right, of course – as she so often is. Occasionally, some of us are fortunate enough to find new and helpful ways of expressing old ideas. But, I certainly must admit that I am the beneficiary of all that has gone on before, around, and indeed within me. Specifically, I acknowledge the influence of my friends in the National Speakers Association. Their acceptance of me and the gift of their example to me have both benefitted my speaking and my writing.

Mission Statement

The mission of *Think Like A Giraffe* is to provide a reach-for-the-sky guide in creativity and maximum performance and to serve as a reminder that people do not have to remain the way they are!

Contents

An Introduction 11

The Direction

I   The "Just One " Principle 19
The Celebrating

II   The "Past Performance" Principle 25
The Stretching

III   The "Gain Forest" Principle 31
The Visiting

IV   The "They Find You" Principle 43
The Knowing

V   The "The FW" Principle 51
The Combining

VI   The "I's Have It" Principle 67
The Pursuing

The Discipline

VII   The "Mind-Tank" Principle 87
The Watching

VIII   The "Goose" Principle 97
        The Pondering
IX   The "Just Like" Principle 105
        The Comparing
X   The "Back Pocket" Principle 113
        The Protecting
XI   The "Eliminate/Duplicate" Principle . . .121
        The Eliminating/Duplicating

The Delight

XII   The "Intellectual Workout" Principle . .133
        The Limbering
XIII   The "Struggle" Principle 137
        The Struggling
XIV   The "S-O-O-S" Principle 153
        The Driving
XV   The "Clogging" Principle 159
        The Clogging
XVI   The "Nothing But Net" Principle 165
        The Being Human
XVII   The "Commencement" Principle 171
        The Commencing
XVIII   Think Like A Giraffe 175
        The Poem

An Introduction

Direction, Discipline, Delight –
these are three keys toward growth in
creativity and performance.
STEPHEN M. GOWER

Come on in! I'd like for you to meet three of my friends – Glance, Trance and Dance. Each is an expert in creativity and maximum performance.

There is a reason why I thought you might like to greet them. I hear, on pretty good authority, that you are keenly interested in raising the level of your creativity and performance. I congratulate you and encourage you at this point.

While many may moan "Why didn't I think of

that?" or "If only I could do that," you are reaching within, up and out, for creativity and performance sparks. Accordingly, it does not surprise me that this book caught your attention, for you see, it is all about reaching.

And, so are Glance, Trance and Dance. Their very being exhudes a commitment to reaching that transcends anything I have ever seen. That is why I wanted you to meet them. So indeed, come on in to the book-house!

You will not be here long before you notice that the *Think Like A Giraffe* book-house is divided into three rooms or three parts. I have asked each of our three honored guests (Glance, Trance and Dance) to serve as a host or hostess, perhaps even a mascot, for a particular room.

Glance will serve as host for room-part one. We call this room DIRECTION. You will notice that the back wall of this room is literally blanketed with posters and pictures of giraffes. And, "look a there" – every giraffe is glancing upward. No incessant pouting is allowed in this room. Creativity and maximum performance certainly allow for some disillusionment and discouragement, but as Glance would say: "You gotta focus on the upward glance – for

Direction...Discipline...Delight

you see, a reach-for-the-sky guide in creativity and maximum performance must begin in a positive and upward DIRECTION!"

The host for room-part two, DISCIPLINE, prefers to be called a mascot. So, let us oblige. Introducing, Trance – your mascot for DISCIPLINE.

There is a reason why Trance prefers the nomenclature of "mascot" over "host." Trance words it this way: "A host is only occasionally in a particular room, often for just a few moments. I want to go where our guests go. Let me be on their bumper stickers, let me be on their refrigerator magnets, let me be on their caps and coats, their watches and umbrellas. For you see, I am a constant reminder. I am a mascot that can become a menace. Focus, commitment, determination, discipline – they are all my mission."

Let me add, for Trance, DISCIPLINE most often seems to be a mission that is highly possible.

The third room-part special! It is not only a delight - it is DELIGHT! Our host for DELIGHT calls himself Dance.

Dance would never want to insinuate that you must go through Glance's and Trance's rooms before you enter his room of DELIGHT. Dance certainly

THINK LIKE A GIRAFFE

values the joy and fun that travel within, not only out from, DIRECTION and DISCIPLINE. In other words, Dance knows that there can be, indeed must be, an occasion of DELIGHT in the journey toward creativity and maximum performance.

It is all interwoven. That is why you notice so few walls between the rooms in this reach-for-the-sky guide. That is why you will observe ten-foot ceilings and an extravagant use of windows in our *Think-Like-A-Giraffe* book-house! DELIGHT is fundamentally a celebration – an extension of DIREC-TION and DISCIPLINE.

You will find that, in format, *Think Like A Giraffe* is ultimately a blend between my books which are segmented into three parts and my sixth book, *The Focus Crisis*, which is comprised of thirty-three stand-alone vingettes. I have remained true to a structure that is framed around three parts, each part, at least initially, crying to be read in sequence with the other parts. Nevertheless, in *Think Like A Giraffe*, the separate parts do hold principles that can actually be read independently, but still connect with and reinforce each other.

Before we get started with our book-house tour, I think it is essential that I share with you where

Direction...Discipline...Delight

I first met Glance, Trance and Dance. My first encounter with these three feisty characters was high up in a tree. For you see, Glance, Trance and Dance are leaves that refuse to live close to the ground. They are the very leaves that feed the gentle giants – the giraffes. They are the essence of reaching and stretching, of thinking in an upward direction, of concentrating in a most determined method, and of dancing with a delight that rivals anything I have ever seen.

With great care, with a delicate handling that illustrates the respect I have for Glance, Trance and Dance, I borrow them from tree's high top, escort them into our book-house, and encourage them to lead you through this reach-for-the-sky guide in creativity and maximum performance.

Well, let's get started with our tour of the *Think Like A Giraffe* book-house. I am excited – I cannot wait for you to meet Glance, Trance and Dance!

Part One

The Direction

Eyes down, bear the frown,
Eyes up, win the crown!
GLANCE

CHAPTER 1

The Just One Principle

The Celebrating

Annoying. Disturbing. Untrue! When I hear those "Just One?" words, normally several times a week, I am tempted to respond with "What do you mean 'Just One?'"

Of course, what they mean to ask is whether or not I am by myself and choose to be seated alone. Often, however, the timbre of their voice indicates this "oneness" as less than normal, less than whole – something that is disappointing to them, and should be disappointing to me.

THINK LIKE A GIRAFFE

To be "Just One" is not a shame. To be "Just One" is a serendipity. To be "Just One" is not a humiliation. To be "Just One" is an honor.

As we embark on our journey into thinking like a giraffe, we can indeed learn a lot from this largest one of all mammals. "Just Oneness" does not deserve a question mark. "Just Oneness" mandates an exclamation point.

For our purposes, "Just Oneness" indicates your uniqueness, your capacity to create, your potential for maximum performance, your ability to reach high into the tree for "the leaves way up there."

This term does not emphasize isolation. In reality, it ultimately affirms unity and diversity. Accordingly, "Just Oneness" does not diminish community – it enhances a sense of community. For when one affirms oneself, he or she actually becomes liberated for an accepting and an affirming of other "Just Ones."

This is why giraffes are respected worldwide as "gentle" giraffes. For sure, when they are provoked, they can utilize their devastating kick to blast you from several different angles. Minus provocation, however, the giraffe is "free enough" and "secure enough" for meekness and uniqueness! The giraffe's "Just Oneness" has for centuries proven to be an asset traveling with an exclamation point, rather than a liability sojourning with a question mark.

We can learn a great deal from the giraffe at this particular point. During our time together, I encourage you to concentrate on your "Just Oneness," to capture it, to channel it, and eventually to celebrate it. Oh the giraffe could have felt "on display," insecure, different from everyone else, and as if he were the only one of a kind. However, the giraffe did not choose to squat and sit on "his pity pot."

Just One!

I probably do not know you by name, but I do know this much. You were designed to soar, not sour. You were created for fulfillment, not total frustration. You were crafted so that you could reach toward the sky, not retreat from it.

This may surprise you, but you have the same number of cervical vertebrae as the giraffe – seven. Oh, you cannot stand fourteen to seventeen feet high, but you can stretch your neck, stick it out toward challenge, and reach for the sky. You can think like a giraffe, or you can hold your thoughts in the gutter. You can birth ideas, or you can bury them. You can stick your neck out towards growth, or you can tuck it in and actually regress.

You can say to yourself: *"I am 'Just One?'"* or, you can say to yourself: *"I am 'Just One!'"* There is a key that determines whether the question mark or the exclamation point follows "Just One."

You are that key! You can determine the direction of your life. You can determine whether or not there will be escalation in your creativity and performance levels.

Certainly, there are serious spiritual considerations here. St. Augustine was certainly right when he exhorted: "I find no rest until I rest in Thee." You even have a choice as to whether or not you will allow Him to help you direct your creativity in an appropriate fashion.

No one else is like you. Just as each giraffe has a highly individual pattern of patches, every pattern different from all others, you have an unmistakable fingerprint and possess a distinctive personality, a marvelous creativity-potential, and a unique performance-possibility!

The Just One Principle

No effort will be made in the *Think Like A Giraffe* book-house to duplicate, clone, or change you. "Just Oneness" is not a plague, a burden, or a barrier. "Just Oneness" is a blessing!

If you will look up toward the possibilities, rather than away from them, if the direction of your thinking will include a glance upwards, rather than a retreat, then you will indeed be able to reach for the sky and "think like a giraffe!"

In Summary:

- "Just Oneness" is not a plague, nor is it a prompting for pouting.
- "Just Oneness" is a privilege and a purpose!
- "Just Oneness" is a promise!
- "Just Oneness" can prompt you to "think like a giraffe."
- Your direction will not "feel right" until it is at one with His direction for you.
- The direction of your thinking determines your decisions.
- The direction of your decisions determines your development.

THINK LIKE A GIRAFFE

- The direction of your development never has to remain stagnant.
- "Just Oneness" is something to celebrate!
- You are someone to be celebrated!
- The direction begins with the celebration!

The fundamental activity of Chapter One in our guide is – *celebrating!*

Reminder Formula:
Your creativity and your performance levels equal your capacity to celebrate your "Just Oneness!"

CHAPTER 2

The Past Performance Principle

The Stretching

Past performance is not indicative of future results.

The statement above normally is included in a prospectus for an investment institution. In most cases, federal and state regulations mandate that investors be cautioned against firmly basing their expectations on prior, and presumably positive, growth percentages.

For our purposes, however, these words greet us not with a caution; they gift us with a challenge.

Certainly we are warned against resting upon

the leaves that we have already discovered – those close-to-the-ground leaves that can indicate our prior accomplishment. However, a more emphatic and exciting interpretation of their meaning causes us to stretch our necks and to remember: things and people do not have to remain the way they are.

If one is to follow a reach-for-the-sky guide toward creativity and maximum performance, then he or she must be open to, and excited about: (1) his or her "Just Oneness" *(the celebration)* and (2) the fact that past performance is not indicative of future results *(the stretching)*. Here, "the stretching" equals a "moving beyond" past performance – a stretching away from past performance.

You should be excited here. For here, you and I are reminded that we, and the things around us, do not have to stay the way they are. Just as a newborn giraffe can grow as much as nine inches in a single week, you and I can lunge out of prior creativity and performance boundaries. Just as the normally gentle and graceful giraffe can aggressively kick himself out of trouble, you and I can, with our Heavenly Father's help, kick ourselves out of the discouragement that can travel along with past performance.

The opportunities for stretching your creativity

The Past Performance Principle

and maximum performance are normally found within the habitat that I call "The Gain Forest" – that lush environment where creativity and performance can thrive. The Gain Forest is that crucible that constantly reminds us that past performance is not indicative of future results.

We can do things to destroy our Gain Forest, just as our world is doing things to destroy The Rain Forest, and we will certainly be visiting our destructive maneuvers. However, for now, let us state how important it is to preserve our Gain Forest – that delightful haven for creativity and maximum performance. Remember, this haven always keeps this sign on out front for you – "past performance is not indicative of future results!"

We will be visiting The Gain Forest in the next chapter, but for now, let me remind you that it is one of Glance's favorite places. For you see, The Gain Forest is all about an upward direction – a direction beyond past performance, a direction possible because of a reach-for-the-sky attitude.

Here, reaching transcends the celebration that travels along with "Just Oneness" to include the stretching that leads one beyond past performance into higher levels of creativity and performance.

THINK LIKE A GIRAFFE

You and I are very aware that stretching exercises can enable us to reach peak physical performance. Well, stretching exercises can also help raise our creativity and performance levels.

STRETCH

1. Stretch your eyes! Roll your eyes around in your head. See new possibilities. See sights you missed as a child.
2. Stretch your neck! Imagine you possess a very long neck. See your stretched-out neck, blessed with both courage and grace, reaching for those leaves high up in the tree. Imagine an upward direction, a firm discipline, a serendipitous delight.
3. Stretch your legs! Stretch them in different ways. Imagine you have four legs, rather than two. If you had four legs, how would you walk? Would you walk like the giraffe – two by two, side by side? Where can your legs take you that you have not gone before? From what "past performance" will your legs help you depart?

"Will Be" Over "As Is"

As long as we choose "as is" over "will be," we will be missing massive opportunities for growth. Please, never allow yourself to escape this truth. A fundamental tenet of this guide in creativity and maximum performance is this – *you cannot go where you want to go – and stay where you are – at the same time!*

If Chapter One was all about celebrating your "Just Oneness," then Chapter Two is about stretching beyond your "As Isness." At this point, the direction of your thinking must recognize the importance of both the celebration and the stretching.

In Summary:

- Past performance is not indicative of future results.
- People and things do not have to remain the way they are.
- We can learn a great deal from The Gain Forest.
- Stretching your eyes, neck, and legs will

prepare you for growth – for your visit
into your Gain Forest.
- You cannot go where you want to go –
and stay where you are – at the same time.

The fundamental activity of Chapter Two in
our guide toward creativity and maximum performance is – *stretching!*

Reminder Formula:
"As Is" minus the stretching equals "As Is."

CHAPTER 3

The Gain Forest Principle

The Visiting

A ny guide into creativity and maximum performance must include a thorough exploration of The Gain Forest.

There is a turf out there, beautiful beyond comprehension. I call her The Gain Forest – or "terra potentia." Blessed with soil that rivals any pile of compost, gifted with an eclectic blending of the air and the light and the wet, she sprouts and nurtures ideas that equal freshness – not staleness. The Gain Forest performs her ritual within an environment where the emphasis is on reaching for the sky rather than sitting around on the woodland floor.

Those who visit and care for her are greeted with gain. Potential is recognized, absorbed, released. One would think that the mass of women and men would sojourn into this forest, pamper her, commit to her, never abandon her.

Yet many are derelict - insisting on treating this forest of creativity and maximum performance with disrespect. Some choose apathy – passive in nature. Others elect downright destruction – active to the core.

Unfortunately, their responses to The Gain Forest mirror the attitudinal (passive apathy) and behavioral (active destruction) persuasions that many exhibit toward The Rain Forest - that diminishing crucible of aesthetic, medicinal, and many undiscovered benefits.

If what is occurring in The Rain Forest is a tangible illustration of the abuse and waste of materials, then what is happening to The Gain Forest reflects abused and wasted minds. What a shame!

You do not want to be a part of that – do you? A massive smorgasbord of concepts, approaches, and constantly expanding potential stands before us.

The Gain Forest Principle

While many walk by, literally oblivious to the table, others choose to rambunctiously swipe the meat of ideas and the fruit of performance off the table; some merely sample the goods and elect emptiness over fulfillment.

A Better Way

There is a better way! You can swallow and digest more and more from The Gain Forest table. Your extensive visit into the "terra potentia" of your heart and mind can help you increase your idea-inventory and accelerate your productivity.

Time spent in The Gain Forest can help you think like a giraffe. You can reach for the lush wonders up there. You do not have to settle on the "past performance" leaves down there. Your time spent in The Gain Forest can help you transcend where you are – no matter where you are. The Gain Forest can influence the direction of your creativity and performance. Remember, however, issues related to creativity and maximum performance must always be perceived as process – never as event. This is a never-ending process.

A Marriage Between Moments

The whole of our time together in this book-house is about The Gain Forest. New ideas and increased performance exist in The Gain Forest. Growth occurs when you place the highest you know of yourself, at a particular moment, into a state that equals the most you can absorb from The Gain Forest, at a particular moment.

Now – here comes a very important reach-for-the-sky principle. The levels of the "highest you know at a particular time" and the range of the "most you can absorb from The Gain Forest at a particular moment" will fluctuate. Here, even though you should certainly expect occasional regression in the levels of knowledge and in the range of absorption, you must fundamentally celebrate the fact that growth in the areas of creativity and performance will occur.

Sadly, some choose The Wastelands over The Gain Forest. They act as if they have nothing to celebrate, no need to stretch, nothing to gain from visiting this forest of "terra potentia." They say: "Why think like a giraffe? Why reach out for something better? I am too tired, too discouraged, too frustrated!"

The Gain Forest Principle

You Are The Key

If you were to reflect on the past year, would you find that some of your thoughts were centered more in The Wastelands than in The Gain Forest? Were you your greatest discourager? In all honesty now, is it possible that *you* have kept *you* out of The Gain Forest? Have you directed yourself into The Wastelands? Or, have you been traveling in the direction of The Gain Forest?

Of course I cannot answer for you – but I can answer for me. There have certainly been times when the direction of my thinking has led me away from The Gain Forest and into The Wastelands.

I have sought to blame it on institutions and organizations. I tried to hold others and my environment responsible for my leaning toward the direction of The Wastelands. Ultimately, I had to take responsibility for the direction in which my creativity and performance were headed.

When I began to take that responsibility, I began thinking like a giraffe – looking upwards, reaching for the sky, stretching myself out of The Wastelands into The Gain Forest. Earlier, it was of little comfort to me that I was not alone in The

Wastelands. Now, I observe that there are many people in The Wastelands, and I am challenged to encourage them to ponder The Gain Forest.

Quite often, it is the way we interpret and respond to our Wasteland Information that dwarfs our creativity and stifles the direction of our performance.

Wasteland Information

By Wasteland Information, I refer to our incessant negative thinking. In my own life, I have missed countless opportunities for growth because I programmed into my head wrong information about myself. I put more limits into the catalogue of my mind than needed to be there. I created negative ideas. I fed and nurtured those counterproductive ideas with selective and discouraging thinking. Let me give you a specific example.

When I was first contemplating professional speaking on a fulltime basis, I noticed myself pursuing all the reasons I should not follow this new career. I am not talking about that normal cataloguing of "pros and cons" that should accompany any significant decision. Here, I am referring to an incessant

The Gain Forest Principle

obsession with negative or Wasteland Information. When I could not justify my negative thinking with my own experiences, I would turn to the negative experiences of others to discourage me. The negative information that I found from other sources would pile up and I began to lose perspective.

Now, many years later, I am convinced that if I had been looking for positive reasons to pursue professional speaking on a full time basis, I would have found many of them.

I can only state that it is a miracle that I am now doing what I love to do, because I certainly tried to stack the odds against myself with negative, Wasteland Information!

You Will Find What You Are Looking For

The direction of your searching is one of the most important factors in determining the levels of your creativity and performance.

If you are looking for The Wasteland, it is there. If you are looking for The Gain Forest, it is there!

If the giraffe looks for leaves high up in the tree, he will eventually find them. If he looks for an acacia tree, loaded with water, he will eventually find it. If the giraffe is concerned about predators, he can stretch his neck in defensive fashion and find what he is looking for. If this gentle and graceful giant needs to protect himself, or if he needs to protect a baby giraffe, he can look for and find a way to use his devastating kicks.

If you and I want to look for opportunities to reach for higher levels of creativity and performance, we can find them – for we will find what we are looking for.

I have seen it in operation time and time again. A company looks for things that are going wrong. They dwell on them. They live in The Wastelands. The direction of their thinking is counterproductive. They own a negative "thought-life."

However, I work with many other companies who have a penchant for seeing possibilities in the midst of, and in spite of, problems. They have a capacity to dwell on that which is right more than to dwell on that which is wrong. They look for and find: gifts, blessings, growth, progress, creativity, and maximum performance most everyday. For sure, however, there are days of discouragement.

Illusions

"Diplessness" and "awkwardlessness" are illusions. Even giraffes get frustrated. Though the giraffe's sense of bonding is probably not as strong as that of Homo sapiens, one can just imagine how frustrated giraffes become with the loss of their young. Studies indicate that more than two-thirds of the giraffe babies die in their first year, many of them in the early months. Lions, hyenas, crocodiles, cheetahs, leopards, and diseases, as well as human poachers, take their toll on baby giraffes. So, even the apparently positive, upbeat, graceful, and "sky-reaching" giraffe can be frustrated.

However, those of us who have been fascinated with this gentle, graceful giant certainly perceive him as one who spends more time looking for the positive rather than one looking for the negative.

Up Or Down

You and I can learn a great deal from the giraffe here. The direction of our thinking can be upscale, rather than downscale. We can stumble and still keep our head up – toward the sky.

THINK LIKE A GIRAFFE

Speaking of the giraffe, he is most vulnerable when his head is down – when the direction of his head is toward the ground. When he reveals splayed legs, when he drops his head, and when he has no lookout companion, the giraffe is susceptible to a legion of villains.

As we close this chapter on alternative directions, The Wasteland or The Gain Forest, let me share a personal illustration.

It is routine for me to fly toward Atlanta after a just-completed speech. Quite often, I will have in my briefcase evaluations from the morning's sessions. I am always grateful for the positive feedback, but I, like most speakers, have a penchant for dwelling on any negative feedback. If I am not careful, and quite often I am not, I will dwell on the negative input rather than the positive. I will interpret the evaluations, even though they are 97% positive, three percent negative, in such a way as to discourage myself.

I know much better. I know that, just as I encourage our clients to give most of their time to the most of their people who utilize most of their strengths, so should I be giving most of my time to celebrating, and even further chiseling, my existing strengths. I do not always do that. Sometimes, I inappropriately interpret the evaluations in such a way as to create my own Wasteland. And, do you know what happens? I miss The Gain Forest.

I do not want you to do that. I do not want you to miss The Gain Forest. I want you to visit your Gain Forest. Reach. Search. Adventure. Explore. Do not do yourself in. Get out of The Wasteland Thinking. The Gain Forest is something to be visited! But, you must look up – toward your sky!

In Summary:

- There's a wonderful place out there – it's called The Gain Forest!
- We can ignore, destroy, or protect The Gain Forest.
- To ignore or destroy The Gain Forest is to retreat from higher levels of creativity and performance.
- The Gain Forest equals an inventory of ideas.
- The Gain Forest equals an inspiration from companions.
- The Gain Forest equals "terra potentia."

- Growth occurs when you commit the highest you know of yourself, at a particular moment, to the highest you know about your Gain Forest, at a particular moment.
- The range of commitment – "the highest of self to the highest of The Gain Forest" – fluctuates.
- We determine the direction of our thinking – Wasteland or Gain Forest?
- The Gain Forest is where passion, conviction, creativity, and maximum performance can find you. Visit your Gain Forest.

The fundamental activity of Chapter Three is – *visiting.*

Reminder Formula:
The Gain Forest minus the visiting
equals The Wasteland.

CHAPTER 4

The They Find You Principle
The Knowing

If raising the levels of your creativity and performance is the issue, then the direction of your thinking should be toward *celebrating*, *stretching* and *visiting*. But, there is much more.

I intentionally referred to the "they find you" principle in the very last part of our preceding chapter. You will recall my referring to The Gain Forest as that place where passion, commitment, creativity, and maximum performance can find you.

THINK LIKE A GIRAFFE

It is the thinking of anyone familiar with human resource development that passion, purpose, a reason for it all, must precede any ultimate growth in the areas of creativity and maximum performance. Whatever the direction of your thinking and doing, "your why" must be blessed with purpose and passion. You must have "your why" together, before you will be able to bring "your what" to ultimate fruition.

When I say the "why" must precede the "what" and the "when" and the "where" and the "how," I am not alone! You can certainly exhibit behavior without passion, but for the most part it will be behavior emanating out of The Wasteland, not out of The Gain Forest. You can certainly have appropriate behavioral responses to all that is occurring within and around you, but if there is to be intensity within the behavior, then your attitudinal response must be one of passion. Again, this is not unusual thinking.

What is unusual is this! I prefer to suggest that we are most creative and come closest to maximum performance, not necessarily when we find passion, but when passion first finds us! It is my strongly held opinion that passion, commitment, creativity and maximum performance come together the most effectively within, and out from us, when passion and commitment initiate the first encounter, rather than when we initiate the first encounter.

Worded another way, we are always hearing that if we want to do something well, we must find confidence. I am not sure this is correct. If we are to do something well, confidence must first find us! Put your arms around purpose and you can succeed. Let purpose put her arms around you and you can soar!

We must cooperate! Our capacity to receive purpose's initiative is terribly important. Our capacity to receive from purpose and passion is a great gift we share with ourselves.

If you really want to think like a giraffe, if you want to exhibit an attitudinal and behavioral reach-for-the-sky approach, then you must glance with your whole person in a direction that will allow passion to come in touch with you.

Form Versus Force

But how do you do that? If allowing passion to find you may be more helpful in raising your creativity and performance levels than your first finding passion, then precisely what is the difference between your finding passion – and passion finding you?

It may be the difference between your creativity and performance levels staying where they are – or your creativity and performance levels reaching new peaks! It could well be the difference between form and force!

It could also be the difference as expressed in the following: "I believe in this" or "This believes in me." "I can get to love this" or "This loves me." "This is who I am" or "This is who I can be." Now do not misunderstand me here. Surely, we all agree that the purpose we find can enhance our thinking and our performance. But, sometimes when it occurs in this fashion, when we find the purpose, there can be a shallowness, an inconsistency, low levels of performance, or even an artificiality that is not present when purpose is so powerful as to overtake us.

Have you not seen that happen to a person? I have.

It was in Atlanta – two months ago. I was at Chastain Park – one of our country's great open-air concert halls. About dusk, a presence touched the platform and transformed the entire arena. You could argue with me for months that this person sang with such power because she found her passion. But, I would never be convinced. No, Celine Dion sang her heart out because passion – "the song," "the singing" – first found her. Celine Dion had it – because it first found her. It found her with a *force* that would not let go.

You Cannot Give What You Do Not Have!

Now the real issue is this: how do you know when passion has found you? Well I could say that it is more real, more natural, more exciting, more fulfilling, and more conducive to higher levels of creativity and performance! And then you might well say – "More than what?" And, I would respond, "More than form!"

For you see, this is a force over form issue. It is an issue of "getting to the heart of the matter" over "going through the motions." Do you recall that earlier I said that the force that travels with passion finding you is more powerful and natural than the form that is merely an extension of your discovering passion? Let me try to express that another way.

THINK LIKE A GIRAFFE

Your most creative self and your highest levels of performance are not items to be taken off a shelf or artificially infused into your head and heart. Your highest levels of creativity and performance are reached when you connect with that One who first connected with you. You sing most effectively when you are first sung unto. You lead most authentically when you are first led with intensity. You invent software that comes out of your heart because an idea was so powerful to grab hold of you – rather than you merely picking it up and attaching form to it. You forgive when you have first been forgiven.

You paint the ocean only after the ocean's wet and salt have first touched your skin. You paint the ocean only after you have ridden her chariot of waves. You know about the ocean because you have experienced her. You have her – and because you have her, you know her. That is why you can paint her so brilliantly and beautifully. You give her back to us so well because you have her to give.

You will be able to stick your neck out more courageously, to live your life more gracefully, to reach for the sky more authentically, when you genuinely relax. Open yourself up so that you can feel, sense, and respond to that purpose which is not alien to you, but that purpose which is actually a part of you – a part of you calling to you – saying "Singer, sing" or "Lawyer, seek justice" or "Leader, lead" or "Salesman, sell" or "Nurse, serve."

You Will Know

Remember your early conversations with your parents. Perhaps one of those conversations went something like this: "Dad, Mom, I'm just not sure that I will ever know whom I am to marry. How will I ever know who the right one is?" And, your parents probably responded something like this, "Oh, you will know – you will know!" And, you probably said to yourself, and maybe even to them, "Well, that really answered my question."

How will you know when "the why" has captured you, rather than your merely capturing "the why"? Oh, you will know – you will know! And, it will make all the difference in the world in your creativity and in your performance levels. It will have everything in the world to do with the direction of your thinking. It will serve as a solid foundation for the *celebrating* of your "Just Oneness," for your *stretching* beyond past performance, for the *visiting* into your Gain Forest.

Yes, you will know. And, the force of your knowing will transcend the shaky form of any disappointing, past performance.

In Summary:

- In a battle between force and form, force will win!
- The direction of your thinking has everything in the world to do with the force behind your thinking.
- Knowing has a lot to do with growing.
- Artificial or authentic – is that not the question?
- You cannot give what you do not have.
- You will know – you will know.

The fundamental activity of the fourth chapter in our guide is – *knowing!*

Reminder Formula:
The force plus the following
equals the fulfillment.

CHAPTER 5

The FW Principle

The Combining

ou might say that the giraffe is a hybrid – a mixture between a huge camel and a spotted leopard. As a matter of fact, if you were to search for the modern scientific name for the giraffe, you would discover *Giraffa camelopardalis.*

If the giraffe looks like a hybrid, then you and I can think like a hybrid. Here, our hybrid thinking is an extension of the "FW" principle.

This principle reminds us that it takes two. Yes, it takes two FW's to grow. You have two phenomenal arsenals at your disposal. When you are at your most creative self, when you are maximizing your performance, you are actually a hybrid of these two arsenals. Most of us are aware that the two stockpiles exist, but somewhere along growth's awkward way, we forget one of our FW's.

However, if we are to grow our "reach-for-the-skyness," if we are to stretch our performance, we must constantly visit and utilize both of our FW's. To benefit from both is to be in wonder. To ignore either is to wither. The direction of our growth must be that which includes both FW's.

The two basic FW's are *From Within* and *From Without*.

From Within

From Within is what you have been given. At birth, and even as a result of your early growth crucible, you were gifted with abilities, some powerful attitudes, and with some strong tendencies. The abilities, attitudes, and even influence that permeated your very being at birth (yes, you can talk to and influence babies before they are born) forms your first FW – From Within. Very early on, it is an innate, inborn, "from-the-start," part of you. From Within has everything in the world to do with issues we discussed earlier – particularly "just oneness" and the superiority of "a passion finding you" over your finding a passion. Ultimately, your attitude about "just oneness" and "the passion that finds you" must be birthed by you — by your From Within!

From Without

From Without is what you have added, what you have absorbed, soaked in, swallowed, read, breathed, heard, enjoyed, and endured. From Without sometimes wears the face of Easy; on another occasion, it puts on the face of Difficult. At other times, From Without can benefit from that which has gone on before.

From Without can participate in functions of addition and even in tables of multiplication with From Within. From Without can be a beautiful and beneficial place. From Without can actually equal The Gain Forest. But, we must care for From Without and allow her to gallop with From Within – two feet by two feet, side by side, in a fresh, giraffe-like way!

FW Minus FW Equals FW (Number One)

From Within minus From Without equals Frustration Within! Or, one could replace Frustration Within with *Failure Worries*, or *Frustrated in Work*, or *Failure in Work*, or *Future Waffling*. I do believe Frustration Within a superior term because it is all encompassing.

The think-like-a-giraffe point here is this: Focus Within minus Focus Without equals Frustration Within – if your goal is growth in creativity and growth in the level of your performance. Though I doubt if there was ever a time when From Within, on its own, in total isolation, birthed creativity and maximum performance for you and for me, I am certain that time is not now. Even what solved some problems and maximized some opportunities two months ago is already cast as, in giraffe-like-terms, "leaves close to the ground" – if not "leaves already on the ground."

Your From Within is always calling for From Without. Your From Within will always be less effective, less creative, more inclined to lower levels of performance, when you do not gift her with the plethora of personalities and experiences which I call From Without – the external blessings that enhance your internal given.

To raise the levels of one's creativity and performance is to point oneself in a direction that seeks and appropriately responds to From Without.

From Without is an imposing creature. Just look at all the patches on her large, tall body. From Without, like her friends, the giraffe and The Gain Forest, knows to look for ideas in the right places. With these ideas, she can create programs, toys, events, product, medicines, sermons, lessons, software, medical procedures, sales results – experiences that supersede levels of prior performance.

Let me list for you some of the faces of From Without – some idea-starters and possible performance-maximizers. Naturally, every one of these may not be appropriate for you and your situation, but perhaps at least one is! And, that could be enough!

From Without's Faces:

Advertisements	Listen, read, watch as many as you can.
Bulletin Board	Utilize a cupboard of ideas shared by your team.
Competition	This will surprise you.
Dictionaries	Dictionaries prove to be great "idea-starters."
Encyclopedias	Consider these expanded dictionaries.
Friends	Particularly value those who care enough to disagree.
Grandparents	If you are blessed enough to still have them with you, listen and learn.
Humor	Enjoy the humor of another and allow it to birth ideas within you.
Inquire	Ask question after question. Become a "questioneer."
Journey	Other cultures will spawn ideas for you.
Keep	Keep a journal of what you observe (though related to

The FW Principle

	"From Within," this journal can be of immense value to your creativity and performance).
Library	Your second or third home it may become.
Method	Observe the methods of others for idea starters.
Networking	The net works if you work the net.
Operating Manuals	Learn as much as you can about how other things work.
Probe	Probe the Internet for ideas.
Quickly	Read book summaries.
Retirees	They may prove to be your grandest "From Without" source.
Subscribe	Benefit from trade magazines and other publications.
Taste	Choose food which inspires alertness, not food which triggers dullness.
Utilize	Take advantage of your existing library.

THINK LIKE A GIRAFFE

Volunteer	Learn from a Boy's Club or Girl's Club member.
Watch	Observe the heart within a high school athlete at play.
Xylophone	Let music ignite your creativity.
Yearn	Desire to be with those superior to you in your field.
Zoom	Zoom or surf or browse technocracy.

FW Minus FW Equals FW (Number Two)

Before we examine what "FW Plus FW Equals FW" means, let us explore another interpretation of the "FW Minus FW Equals FW" formula.

Earlier, we stated that From Within minus From Without equals Frustration Within. We must now explore the other side of the jungle of frustration here – when From Without minus From Within equals Frustration Within. Here, we are aware of, and even minimally responsive to the plethora of the faces of From Without – however, we are not fully cooperating with From Without.

The FW Principle

Why is this? When it comes to our creativity and our performance levels, why is our From Within reticent, refusing to stretch, oblivious to the possibilities of growth, apathetic about the elimination of The Gain Forest, so unconcerned about the extension of thinking-like-a-giraffe?

There are several reasons which explain one's significant reluctance to supplement From Without with From Within. For our purposes, each reason falls under the umbrella called attitude.

You will recall that on page 52, I included attitude in a description of From Within. I am aware that there are those who choose to separate attitude from the given. They would not assign attitude to From Within. I not only choose to include attitude in what I call From Within, I perceive attitude as the most important patchwork on From Within's body.

Deep within oneself is the ability to fret or to focus, to pout or to polish, to sulk or to sculpt. One can choose the attitude that equals aloofness or one can choose the attitude that equals alertness. One's stance toward the leaves close to the ground or one's stance toward the leaves high in the trees, one's tilting toward a pursuit of The Wasteland or one's significant journey into The Gain Forest, equals one's attitude.

THINK LIKE A GIRAFFE

When we choose excessive caution or callousness over creativity, when we choose excessive preoccupation, even fascination and incomprehensible satisfaction with mediocrity over maximizing performance, we falter. We exhibit the attitude that chokes and stifles the expansion of our inventory of ideas and thwarts any progress toward optimum achievement.

Our attitude is actually depriving From Without any assistance by our From Within. If you are to think like a giraffe, then you must reach toward the sky with all of your heart and mind. You must allow From Within to befriend From Without.

Negative Attitudes

Negative Attitudes are destroying The Gain Forest – that precious haven of lush ideas and thriving performance discussed in Chapter Three. Negative Attitudes are giving birth to Wastelands – eclectic gatherings of worn-out ideas and wasted food for thought. Negative "From Within" Attitudes say: "It cannot get any worse than this." They see only those leaves close to the ground or already on the ground. Negative Attitudes just never seem to be able to put the pieces together.

Positive attitudes, however, those that emphasize an upward, reach-for-the-sky direction, actually nurture creativity and performance. Oh, certainly there will be some frustration, some disappointment and ambiguity. "Ambiguitylessness" is an illusion. The positive attitude that is such a vital ingredient in From Within does not travel without or away from frustration, it sojourns through frustration.

Analyze your level of frustration in your negative and positive attitudes. You will probably find levels of frustration present in both. But, here comes your think-like-a-giraffe point here – the frustration factor is much higher in a negative attitude than it is in a positive attitude. For some, excessive frustration will take the beauty out of The Gain Forest. Negative Attitude wins.

For others, frustration, though initially biting with disappointment, actually elicits the finest creative juices and optimum performance. Positive attitude wins – even though the winning may not look like what one initially hoped it would be, or thought it would be.

If frustration equals a huge "where I have been" factor, then "where I have been" can totally stop some. However, it actually seems to propel others.

They approach maximum performance not only in spite of, but quite often because of, the "where I have been" factor. Again, your think-like-a-giraffe point here is this – "your frustration may be your grandest tutor when it comes to creativity and performance."

Negative Attitude allows frustration with the "where I have been" factor to serve as a leech that attaches itself to From Within and permeates From Within to the point of perceived, if not real, dysfunction.

It Does Not Have To Stay Like It Is

If Negative Attitude has hold of us, then we must remember this, it does not have to stay like it is! There is a way in which From Within and From Without can meet each other, grow to like each other – masterfully create and perform with each other. There is a way for From Within and From Without to join forces and together think-like-a-giraffe. There is a method for From Within and From Without to unite and reach-for-the-sky together. There is a way for this powerful duo, From Within and From Without, to preserve and enjoy The Gain Forest.

The FW Principle

Together, they can replace a minus with a plus!

What will it take? It will take a Positive Attitude. Without Positive Attitude, there will always be Frustration Within – either frustration birthed by the absence of From Within or frustration created by the absence of From Without. But, when they join forces, when From Within and From Without unite, there is victory over dominant frustration; there is growth in creativity and maximum performance.

Has your Negative Attitude kept you down? Has your "where you have been" got the best of you – stifled your energy, smothered your spirit? Is your thought-life not as positive as it used to be, not as sharp as it used to be, because of dominant frustration? Remember, it does not have to stay like it is. But, you must think-like-a-giraffe – you must hold to a positive reach-for-the-sky attitude. And, sometimes, that may mean sticking your neck out – into The Gain Forest!

FW Plus FW Equals FW

From Within (a Just Oneness gifted with a Positive Attitude) plus From Without (a stretching into the huge reservoir that is The Gain Forest) equals

THINK LIKE A GIRAFFE

Fulfillment Within.

Oh, it certainly equals Focus Within and Fun Within as well, but once again, I perceive the chosen term as all inclusive. For, when one is at his or her most creative self (here I must add – in a close, non-separated relationship with the Creator) – when one is in the process of maximizing performance (here I stress – process, not event) – when one is found by focus and fun too (here I emphasize – found by), that one knows what fulfillment and satisfaction and meaning look like.

When From Within and From Without marry each other, they give birth to creativity, to performance that is being maximized, to Fulfillment Within. They may encounter rough times. Often, the sense of fulfillment only begins to materialize after their marriage goes through the jungle of a rocky start. But ultimately, as each matures, there is more to celebrate – fewer justifications for constantly complaining.

I invite you to take a ride in your FW – really your two FW's – From Within and From Without. Are you really taking advantage of both? Does hesitation reign supreme? When is the last time you've driven your FW's into The Gain Forest? Do you have

the courage to stick your neck out? Are you exhibit-
ing a Negative Attitude or a Positive Attitude?
Remember, it is this very attitude that is the most significant variable in From Within. Remember, this is
where you play a crucial role in your own creativity
and performance!

In Summary:

- From Within minus From Without equals
  Frustration Within.
- From Without minus From Within equals
  Frustration Within.
- From Within plus From Without equals
  Fulfillment Within.
- The direction of your thinking must be
  combined – both From Within and
  From Without.

The fundamental activity of Chapter Five is –
combining.

Reminder Formula:
It takes two, From Within plus From Without,
to equal Fulfillment Within!

CHAPTER 6

The I's Have It Principle

The Pursuing

If you are familiar with my third book, *Celebrate The Butterflies – Presenting With Confidence In Public,* you are aware that a significant section of that book deals with the importance of eye contact. A broad heading for that issue is: "The Eyes Have It."

For this book, and in this section I am addressing a totally different subject – not your eyes that help you make contact with your audience and invite them in to "TouchSpeech," but the five "I's" that serve as catalysts for creativity, the five "I's" that can point you in an upward direction, a reach-for-the-sky direction toward higher levels of creativity and performance.

For our purposes, the five "I's" are: Inspiration, Interpolation, Introspection, Isolation, Imagination. Each must be pursued.

Inspiration

Nature can certainly spawn creativity: golden leaves riding on wind's chariot into a pond of quiet, Daddy Bluebird proudly standing guard for Mama, the redbud's leaves of heart, the river birch's peeling bark, hostas that harmonize with ferns of cinnamon, a covey of quail fleeing from a frustrated squirrel, an ocean forest of kelp, the phenomenal molting of the lobster, the salmons' sojourn of struggle against the current, cotton-ball puffs of clouds, a massive mirror named Salt Lake, a night in the woods with cold's call for campfire, a wealth of water careening down a structure of rocks – falling into a pool that becomes a river that segments itself into a series of streams, the marvelous cycle of seasons which inspires one who values how naked limbs produce lush leaves that later die only to soon nourish naked limbs again,

The I's Have It Principle

and ultimately the birth of a child and the rebirth of a man and a woman.

Inspiration's source lies not only within nature's nurturing and resting places, inspiration's catalyst can appear on paper – a book by Zig Ziglar, a poem by Maya Angelou, a novel by Og Mandino, a painting by Andrew Wythe. Inspiration can be birthed by an experience in song with Celine Dion, an item of software that carries your computer to new heights of performance, a taped message from your loved one.

God's amazing love for you may of course be your ultimate source of inspiration. When you allow silence to permeate your being, you may position yourself for ultimate inspiration.

For years, I have been sharing with audience members, and with my readers, my strongly held conviction that one cannot motivate another person. Ultimately, motivation must come from within. But, I am certainly acutely aware that one person can inspire another person – help create an environment where the other person is encouraged to motivate himself or herself.

This has certainly been my experience in the National Speaker's Association. I have been inspired by a multitude of giants in our industry, persons who are also my friends: Robert Henry blessing me with the humor that he heaves from his huge heart, Rosita Perez touching me with her passion, Willie Jolly blessing me with his gift of voice, Mike McKinley gifting me with his insight, Bruce Wilkinson inspiring me with his energy. *Pursue introspection.*

Interpolation

When I use the term "interpolation" as one of the five catalysts for creative thinking – one of the five "I's," I am of course visiting the discipline of mathematics and its concept of Interpolation.

As a matter of fact, this very section is a modeling of Interpolation. I am actually illustrating here what I am addressing here. Many of my clients and audience participants will document that Interpolation is actually a source of creativity for them. An event occurs and sparks an idea. Interpolation occurs. One concept actually ends up igniting an extension, a modification, a metaphor, an analogy. One interpolates from the previous and creates that which follows.

The I's Have It Principle

This is not duplicating. It is developing. It is not replicating.

It may resemble "just like thinking" – that powerhouse principle that I will visit in a later chapter. It can be revolutionary.

The direction of your thinking should be aimed in such a fashion as to include Interpolation. Interpolation is worth your visitation if you seriously want to think like a giraffe – and, there I go, interpolating, again! *Pursue interpolation.*

Introspection And Isolation

This segment is being written aboard a Delta Jet headed for Atlanta. I have just completed addressing an International Association of Corrections Trainers. I inquired about their creativity sources – their catalysts. I received two responses which illustrate the point of consideration here. Worded in simple terms, these are the two responses: (1) I am more creative when I experience and reflect upon frustration. (2) I am more creative when I celebrate and reflect upon accomplishment. Each response emanated from Introspection.

Frustration Reflection

I think in most cases "failure" is much too harsh a term. Appropriate phrases might include the following: "reflection on a disappointment," "evaluation of mistakes," "loss review," "an introspection that can help me learn from this," and "traveling by detour." For our purpose, "frustration reflection" is most appropriate.

With that said, reflection on your "where-you-have-been" can ignite ideas heretofore unexplored. The introspection prompted by discouragement and disappointment can actually yield significant deposits into your creativity bank.

What Does Frustration Reflection Look Like?

In my experience, the introspection that is prompted from disappointment or discouragement may have been caused by a single occurrence or a mixture of events. To pursue introspection in relationship to this disappointment or discouragement is to seek to recognize the frustration precipitators.

The I's Have It Principle

Of course I cannot do this for you. This introspection is very personal. But I can share with you what I have learned over the years about frustration precipitators.

First of all, there must be something about which to reflect. There is normally something that precipitates this feeling of disappointment – this sensation of discouragement follows.

Hopefully, the sensation and feeling of disappointment and discouragement is followed by a the search for the precipitator. What did I do that led to the feeling? If one does not participate in this initial stage of Frustration Recognition, then one cannot pursue Frustration Reflection.

You may be concerned with the direction of your creativity and performance – yet unaware of your frustration precipitators. Accordingly, it may be helpful for me to share with you a listing of reasons why many people feel they miss the mark and fall short of their creativity and maximum performance expectations.

A Sampling Of Frustration Precipitators:

- reluctance to consider all the options,
- haste equaling waste,
- impurity of motive,
- insincerity,
- an unvisited library,
- isolation from others,
- temper tantrums,
- inadequate preparation,
- time constraints,
- fear of failure,
- fear of success,
- failure to service one's own journey,
- incessant comparison to others,
- tunnel vision,
- reluctance to commit,
- focusing only on leaves close to the ground,
- too much to do,
- excessive pouting,
- no second opinion inquiry,
- concerns of a spiritual nature.

The I's Have It Principle

Isolate Your Frustration Precipitators

Remember, the key think-like-a-giraffe point here is this: you must first Isolate Your Frustration Precipitators before you can do something about them. But, once these precipitators are recognized and isolated, you can:

- begin the process of growth – (remember growth is not event),
- transcend the vague and approach the verifiable – specificity is the key,
- imagine the improvement in your creativity and performance,
- celebrate your "just oneness" and explore "just likeness."

The introspection that emanates out from Frustration Reflection can certainly position you for growth in the levels of your creativity and performance!

Accomplishment Reflection

When I ask audience participants what encourages them to be most creative, I sometimes get an answer that can be summed up in this fashion:

"I am often most creative when I celebrate, indeed retreat, into prior accomplishments or strengths. My 'after the fact' reflection of an earlier accomplishment actually excites me about future accomplishments. I know I can do something well, and I seek to build upon that which I already do well."

I view this not as a reluctance to do the difficult. It need not be an excessive desire to do only what comes more naturally or more smoothly. I view this as a most creative way to self-start – again.

For example, the giraffe knows he has an advantage in the area of height. That is why he continues to reach for the sky – for those leaves high up there – the leaves that most cannot touch.

A retreat into excellence can breed growth. Celebration of prior achievement can ignite interest in additional, albeit difficult, achievement.

Yes, it could all lead to a perpetual laziness. But here we are addressing the celebration of prior achievement and retreat into what one does well as a launching pad for additional creativity and maximum performance. Please remember that this alternative is far superior to the "mission avoided" outcome that occurs when one denies himself or herself the creative catalyst of positive reflection.

What Does Accomplishment Reflection Look Like?

It may look like the following: "How was I able to do that? In the past it would not work, what made it work this time? Is there anyway that I can take the strength that set this successful event apart from prior failures and even improve upon it? If I isolate the strength or strengths that make it all come together (gestalt), will I be able to duplicate it and indeed create a higher model on a much larger scale?"

This is precisely what happens when a professional speaker seeks to build skills in humor. In one instance, a favorite story seemed to work to illustrate a particular point. In another instance, the story was a total flop.

The professional speaker dwells on the first experience. His or her positive reflection enables the presenter to recognize the difference between A and B, to reflect about why there was a difference, to respond with a "strength-sculpting" that chisels the story here, modifies it there. It is this positive reflection that may mandate the further extension of this story through a pause here, lower volume here, and an escalated pace here. Remember, the story merits and mandates reflection because, to start with, it was such a very good story.

This Accomplishment Reflection phase of introspection becomes cyclical in nature – so that, with some exception, there is ideally growth piled upon growth, improvement piled upon improvement. Again, there will be some regression. Accomplishment Reflection results in a beneficial process, not event.

To summarize our emphasis on the "accomplishment reflection" side of introspection, let me encourage you to ponder for yourself the reality that most of us are most creative when we are sculpting our strengths. Surely, some of the time we, like the giraffe, have to grapple with those leaves so close to the ground. Sometimes, in spite of all of our protective devices, we get hurt on the acuia trees of life. However, like the giraffe, we can focus on our leaves high up in the tree – the strengths we can clearly see, the potential that is more obvious because of the background of a grand, clear sky.

Accomplishment Reflection encourages you to continue, even increase, your reach-for-the-sky efforts – understanding that even if you do not go all the way, you may very likely go far enough to be among the stars, or at least among the giraffes. *Isolate your accomplishment precipitators.*

Though it was referred to in the prior section, I deem it important enough to warrant a risking of redundancy at this point. So, let me emphasize again that which is such a crucial part of our guide. Those who increase the upward direction of their creativity and performance know how to isolate and minimize or eliminate frustration precipitators. They also know how to isolate and duplicate or expand accomplishment precipitators – their gifts, strengths, reach-for-the-sky attitudes, and think-like-a-giraffe behavior. *Pursue introspection and isolation.*

Imagination

The untapped portion of the mind's eye, the uncharted segment of the heart's circulatory course, the sinew behind every imaginable muscle all cry for something new. The spirit's most intense and authentic nature sings a fresh song that crescendos into imagination!

Creative juices ooze, then flow. Vision breeds mission. Mission yields to completion. Completion is transformed into celebration!

Taken too far, of course, all of this "imagination" talk can equal nothing but illusion. It certainly does not always unfold like the scenario described in the prior paragraph. Sometimes, the imagination that runs wild illustrates the point that we are referring to time and again in this book: *any strength taken too far can equal a weakness.*

Imagination can actually give birth to bad, unworkable, hurtful ideas. Bad ideas may lead to stagnation, or to regression, or even to guilt. The imagination that runs wild may run away from reality. The imagination that runs wild may create for the individual a head-on collision. The head-on collision may look like this: disappointment, discouragement, financial chaos, broken promises, ambiguity, The Wasteland. Imagination can certainly equal an ending, or the ending.

However, imagination can equal a tremendous and beautiful beginning – or even an amazing continuing. Imagine what you will discover about yourself when you reach for the sky. Take the completed and celebrated concept that would have been birthed by your creative vision and imagine it a reality!

Visualize what this completion, this celebration, actually looks like. Imagine that you have already received what you are searching for. Envision yourself reaching toward the sky and being held by that for which you are reaching.

Please remember, imagination will strike fear in characters called stagnation, boredom and minimum performance. Imagination is a catalyst for growth in creativity and performance. *Pursue imagination!*

In Summary:

- The direction of your thinking will be positively gifted by appropriate inspiration. This inspiration may cause you to say something like this: "If she can do that under those circumstances, then maybe I can do this under these circumstances."
- Interpolation can remind you to hold to an upward glance – to maintain a positive

direction. Interpolation may gift you in such a way that you will end up saying: "With a different tweak, with a minor or major modification, this type of thinking will work here. If that will work there, why would it not work here?"

- There are two types of introspection – Frustration Reflection and Accomplishment Reflection. You can learn from each type.
- Isolation of frustration or accomplishment precipitators can lead to minimization or elimination of frustration precipitators. It can also lead to duplication or expansion of accomplishment precipitators.
- Envision what you're reaching for actually grabbing hold of you. Allow it to bless the direction of your thinking and behavior in a positive and creative way.
- Pursue: inspiration, interpolation, introspection, isolation and imagination.

The I's Have It Principle

The fundamental activity of Chapter Six is – *pursuing*.

The Reminder Formula is:
Inspiration plus Interpolation plus Introspection
plus Isolation plus Imagination equals
Improvement in Creativity and Performance.

Part Two

The Discipline

*Man and woman most wise know the answer
lies not in procrastination. Neither does
accomplishment swell and sprout from mere
fascination. No, creativity, and performance
too, grow within a soil called determination.*

TRANCE

CHAPTER 7

The Mind Tank Principle

The Watching

Idea *lessness* is a disease. It matters not whether the disease is acute or chronic. In either instance, a firm resolve, a determined discipline, must be an intricate part of one's rehabilitation and recovery. This is also the case if the disease is inappropriate "as isness." Again, discipline must precede that which follows. In this situation, a disciplined commitment to transcend inappropriate "as isness" must come before escalated performance levels.

The Ten Percent Theory

For decades I have been agreeing with them. Why, I have even been saying it myself – "Most of us utilize less than ten percent of our brain."

Well, I am beginning to think that I was not looking at the total picture. My earlier thinking flowed like this: *We are not as creative as we could be, we do not come close to approaching our maximum performance level, because we simply use so little of our mind!*

Minimal Use

The reason, for our low levels of creativity and performance appeared to be related to minimal use of the mind. Seemingly, we were operating on a low "mind-tank" because of minimal use. The theory followed this vein of thinking. Most of our "mind-tank" was going to waste simply because we were choosing not to use it!

At this writing, I continue to respect the validity behind the relationship between creativity and performance and basic mind-use. However, there is much more to our current creativity and maximum performance vacuum than minimal use.

The Mind Tank Principle

Minimal use of one's mind-tank rarely travels alone. Significant misuse of one's mind-tank often sojourns with minimal use. Now one could argue that there is no way that this could occur within the same person. Of course it can. It has happened within me.

I would certainly agree, however, that normally the two issues, minimal use and misuse, are most often highlighted, not within one person, but within an environment that includes many persons.

Retreat from creativity and withdrawal from maximum performance is a reality for some of us because we use so little of our mind-necks. We do not stick them into books. We do not stick them into travel. We do not stick our mind-necks into libraries or concerts, or second opinions or The Gain Forest. We choose to use so very little of what we have.

Misuse

Others of us, however, fall prey to abuse or misuse, not minimal use. Our fuel tank stays on "low" or almost "empty" because we abuse or misuse our creative fuels or juices. Optimum performance is a rare and strange passenger in our life-vehicles. The

THINK LIKE A GIRAFFE

energy with which our fuel gifts us has been mis-spent. *We have creativity and performance problems because of misuse.*

Let me be specific. Let me assume that you are a leader. There are twenty people on your team. Your team has been assigned a standard of performance – to produce one hundred quality pieces of furniture a day.

Fifteen of the team members are performing superbly. Five of the team members are causing problem after problem. They seem to complain all the time, will repeatedly be late for work, will make mistake after mistake, and will exhibit little common sense. You currently label this an issue of their misuse of mindpower. "If the team is to reach or exceed its standard, then these five must carry their weight," you say. So you focus your energy from your fuel tank on these five.

We are talking about a slow and insidious process here, but eventually you notice that you are giving more and more of your time to the perceived "mind misusers." You have almost forgotten about the other fifteen.

You begin to suspect that you have been derelict toward the other fifteen. So, you decide to catalogue your time. And, what you find is this: the one-fourth of the team, the mind misusers, who frustrate you so much, are occupying three-fourths of your time. This, of course, leaves you with one-fourth of your time being given to three-fourths of your superior workers.

You remember that growth, within individuals and within businesses, occurs not through excessive weakness confrontation, but through "particularized" strength affirmation and win reviews. You recognize you are only giving one-fourth of your time to this most significant journey-surfacing of your most effective teammembers. You start to recognize that you, yes you, are actually misusing your mindpower.

In our hypothetical scenario, your perception is correct. I have certainly made the same mistake.

I know better. I know we do not grow when you are constantly catching us doing wrong and serving nothing but "loss reviews" our way. I know we grow when you affirm us in specific and direct fashion. I know we grow when you gift us with "win reviews."

I know standards are met and exceeded, not only when journey-servicing occurs with minimum

THINK LIKE A GIRAFFE

users, but most emphatically when it occurs with the 75 percent who keep on plugging. I understand the 75 percent's need for "particularized" affirmation, praise, and our presence.

You and I must remember that if we are to be growing in relationship to our creativity and performance levels, then we must hold true to this basic think-like-a-giraffe principle. We are not reaching for the sky, we are not being productive, when we give most of our mind-tank to those few who are constantly causing so much frustration.

I may know your thinking here. Why, I even occasionally think this way myself: "Why mess with those who are doing it well? It seems to me like the best way I can get most out of the team is to give most of myself to those that are not pulling their weight!"

Well, my friend, when we do that, we are literally spinning our wheels. Study after study indicates that individuals and businesses grow on the basis of strength affirmation rather than weakness confrontation. We must be disciplined in our approach here, as we remember that all of this impacts the teammembers and us as well.

I have what I do believe is a very helpful suggestion at this point. Quit focusing on those leaves so close to the ground. Quit focusing on the symptoms of frustration. That is what the people who are not carrying their weight are giving you – they are giving you symptoms of their frustration.

When you play their symptom-game with them, you are stifling your own creativity and performance. As long as you focus on their symptoms, as long as you excessively dwell on their symptoms, you are not only perpetuating their mind misuse, you are actually jumping into the tank of mind misuse with them.

We must all be disciplined in our approach here. We must move beyond a focus that is limited to symptoms. If we are to encourage creativity and maximum performance within our team members, and if we are to exhibit higher and higher levels of creativity and performance ourselves, then we must move beyond a concentration that is centered on symptoms to an effort that focuses on systems.

Chances are good that when you are giving most of your time to the few that are not carrying their weight, you are trying to change symptoms that will never be changed until you begin to address the system. The system that works, when it comes to raising creativity and performance levels, is a system of encouragement – a system of solid, "particularized," strength affirmation and win reviews.

Oh certainly, there will be many times when you will have to care enough to confront that small percentage who repeatedly do not do their part. On occasion, your confrontation will be tutorial in nature. On other occasions, it may have to be stronger than merely tutorial. However, we must remain convinced that the system of strength affirmation is superior to constantly battling symptoms emanating from frustrated team members.

This is not only important for them and your business. This is important for you. It is crucial to your creativity and to your performance levels. This is a classic example of what we are talking about in this chapter.

Follow Your Own Advice

When I am giving so much of my energy toward that which I can do so little about, I am not "not using my brain," I am "misusing my brain." Time and again, our creativity is dwarfed and our performance is stifled because we infiltrate our mind-tank with the kudzu of misuse. Inappropriate use of

The Mind Tank Principle

our mind actually begins to percolate through our whole being. Instead of being creative, we become cold and callous. Instead of being creative, we become cynical and caustic. Give enough of your mind to enough negativity and you will become negative.

You tell your children to be careful with whom they spend their time. Follow your own advice.

Watch

Watch your "mind-tank." Is it too low because of minimal use? Or, is it low because of misuse?

It is possible that your creativity and performance "mind-tank" is actually very low because you misspend or waste so much of it on negative and counter productive attitudinal and behavioral responses. Watch your mind-gauge. Watch for minimal use and misuse warning signals! Be disciplined here! Focus on the watching!

Give the energy of your mind to positive systems rather than negative symptoms – within your team and within yourself. You will find yourself reaching for the sky, thinking like a giraffe, raising your levels of creativity and performance.

THINK LIKE A GIRAFFE

In Summary:

- Your mind-tank may not always be low because of minimal use.
- Your mind-tank may be low because of misuse.
- Are you focusing on negative symptoms or positive systems?
- Are you giving more than three-fourths of your time to the less than one-fourth of your team members who frustrate you?
- Watch your mind-tank gauge.
- Watch for minimal use and misuse warning signals.
- Be disciplined in your watching.

The fundamental activity of Chapter Seven is – *watching!*

Reminder Formula:
The discipline of positive and appropriate "mind-use" systems equals much more than an incessant emphasis on minimal "mind-use" symptoms.

CHAPTER 8

The Goose Principle

The Pondering

Ponder the goose!
Those who think like a giraffe may see and profit from the goose - especially when they learn to model the discipline of the goose.

Most of us are aware that, when geese maneuver their way southward away from winter's harshness, they fly in a "V" formation. There are several virtues behind this "V" formation. Each of these four virtues has tutorial value for us in relationship to our creativity and maximum performance.

The "V" formation virtues for pondering are:
- Optimization
- Oscillation
- Observation
- Obligation

Optimization

There is a cyclical benefit related to the "flapping of the wings" of the goose. When Goose A flaps his wings, Goose B, following right behind Goose A, is gifted with a larger flying capacity than if he were flying independently, or solo.

In similar fashion, Goose C is gifted by Goose B, and Goose D by Goose C. Throughout the formation, there is basically a mutual gifting. Studies indicate that an entire flock of geese, flying in a "V" formation, can surpass the "solo-flying" capacity of each goose flying alone by more than two-thirds.

The principle of "V" formation-flying has great tutorial value for us as we seek to raise our levels of creativity and performance. Sometimes, we do our best thinking, our most beneficial brainstorming, our finest work, when we choose not to go it alone.

The Mind Tank Principle

Certainly, solitude can sow creativity. For sure, the masters have painted on canvas tucked away in a garage, or an attic, where they were "flying solo." Normally, novels are not written and nurtured in a crowded movie theater. Concertos are not crafted in overflowing concert halls.

However, the "V" formation that equals "others thinking and working in front of us and behind us" can encourage us. It is a theme that continues to surface in our time together – "be careful with whom you are flying; those with whom you fly can hold you back, or they can lift you up!"

You must remain determined to fly in formation with positive thinkers. You must hold tightly to your discipline of reaching for the sky. At least occasionally, you will want to fly within a "V" formation. When you fly without the other members of the flock, or when you incessantly fly way behind or even way ahead of other members of the flock, you may be denying yourself maximum performance. You may be depriving yourself of a performance that could perhaps be increased by as much as two-thirds from "flying together." *Ponder optimization.*

Oscillation

A lead goose tires. What does he do? He retreats for rest. Another goose rotates to lead position.

Many of my most creative and most productive clients are exceptionally insightful and effective because they know when to rotate toward the rear for rest. They value the occasional shifting of lead-point status to another.

As they oscillate from an active role to an occasional passive role, they position themselves for at least a modicum of rest. Rest ultimately impacts future creativity and performance in a positive fashion.

How selfish are you with the lead position? Do you always have to be at the top of the "V"? Do you allow rest to breed creativity for you? Do you feel less than whole when you relax?

This summer I visited the San Diego Zoo and was intrigued to observe giraffes at rest, giraffes at calm. Reaching is not always related to neck-stretching and lunging forward. Sometimes, reaching draws from resting. On occasion, reaching's resources are found in the back of the formation – where less effort is called for, where the scenery is different, where

The Mind Tank Principle

someone else carries the lead-point challenge.

How good can you become in the discipline of oscillation – of rotating from front to back? Can you rotate away from excessive activity toward a more passive perusal of the attitude and approach of others? Do you have the capacity to receive as well as the ability to give?

Sometimes, to think like a giraffe means to oscillate like a goose. *Ponder oscillation.*

Observation

A goose decides to forego the formation, to fly away, eventually to fatigue himself. He observes his isolation and tires from battling alone the winds of frustration. He observes the inappropriateness of his departure and returns to the gathering of geese. The flock of his fellows gifts him with renewed energy.

In similar fashion, you and I fly into an isolation that is taken too far, exhibit an independence that borders on self-righteousness, resort to a formation-abandonment that ultimately swallows our creative juices and stifles our productivity. Often, only when our fatigue seems most serious, only when we observe the urgency of the situation, will we return to the flock that gifts us with the example of higher levels of creativity and performance. *Ponder observation.*

Obligation

A struggling goose, wounded by weapon of weather or weapon of man, will wander away from the security of formation's arsenal of fellow geese. A couple of geese will appear obliged to pursue their fallen fellow. If their efforts at help are not fruitful, or if the sickly goose dies, they pursue another formation.

I refer to the obligatory nature of the goose in a positive light here. Those who fly in the "V" formation are loyal to those who fly away from the "V" formation. Here, obligation is not that world of excessive "oughts" and "have to's" that can block us away from creativity and maximum performance.

The obligatory side of the goose is a side that emphasizes discipline, determination, and commitment. It stresses the translation of "a care" which is passive and attitudinal in nature into a "loyal caring" which is active and behavioral in nature. This breed

The Mind Tank Principle

of obligation is worth pondering. It can help another; it can benefit you.

There's something about sticking your neck out for another that can free you away from excessive absorption with self and actually free you up for creativity and maximum performance. Here, pursuit is both obligation and opportunity. *Ponder obligation.*

In Summary:

- We can learn a lot from a goose. Our pondering about a goose can equal profit.
- Sometimes flying together produces higher levels of creativity and performance than flying alone. This is optimization.
- Sometimes to think like a giraffe means to oscillate like a goose.
- To observe the inappropriateness of a particular departure may be the first step back toward creativity.
- There is something about sticking your neck out for another that results in freeing you away from counterproductive selfishness. It can also free you up for higher ranges of creativity and performance.

THINK LIKE A GIRAFFE

The fundamental activity of Chapter Eight in our guide is – *pondering!*

Reminder Formula:
Optimization plus Oscillation plus Observation plus Obligation equals Growth in Creativity and Performance.

CHAPTER 9

The Just Like Principle

The Comparing

This is a chapter you will want to read time and again. I know I plan to do just that – for in my experience one cannot "over remind" oneself about the impact of "Just Like" thinking on creativity and maximum performance.

When it comes to raising my creativity and performance levels, I can think of no single principle that has helped me more than "Just Like" thinking. "Just Like" thinking will merit all the determination, discipline, and commitment you can muster. Again, I know this from decades of personal experience. Before I explain how "Just Like" thinking has gifted me, particularly in relationship to my book titles, let me seek to define "Just Like" thinking – this powerhouse think-like-a-giraffe principle.

To utilize "Just Like" thinking is to analyze the concepts behind the development of A and postulate as to what might occur in B, if these concepts were extended in their application toward B. This is the case even if A and B are, on first observation, totally unrelated. "Just Like" thinking is "associational" thinking.

If you can associate A and B, you will grasp the point more quickly, conceive and develop the new product more easily and effectively, and express yourself more thoroughly. Perhaps it will be helpful if I share with you how I applied the principle of "Just Like" thinking while creating many of my books titles.

In my first book, I wanted to address the impact of a quickly expanding and vastly negative attitude on organizations and individuals. I knew, early on, that I needed a way to explain this phenomenon so my audience participants and readers would understand what I meant.

The Just Like Principle

Accordingly, I titled the book *The Art Of Killing Kudzu – Management By Encouragement.* Basically, what I did was to compare this negative attitude to kudzu – that obstinate, cantankerous and robust vine that grows wild and chokes away the good stuff. I used "Just Like" thinking in my title and in the whole of the book – "just like kudzu grows wild and chokes out the good stuff, so does a negative attitude and behavior choke out relationships, creativity, and higher ranges of performance."

In my third book, *Celebrate The Butterflies – Presenting With Confidence In Public,* I compared the three different reactions to the "butterflies" that harbor over the impatiens at the Gower get-together to the three different reactions that we can have in relationship to our nervous energy, "our butterflies," about speaking in public.

When it comes to literal butterflies, there are three different reactions at the Gower get-together: that of the toddler who tries to catch and kill the butterfly, that of the teenager who ignores the butterfly, that of the grown child who celebrates the color and choreography of the butterfly.

In the book, *Celebrate The Butterflies,* I basically said, "Just like there are three different ways to react to the literal butterflies that hover over the impatiens, so are there three different ways you and I can react to our nervous energy about speaking in public. We can try to catch it and kill it – it will not go away. We can try to ignore it – it will not work. Just like the grown child, we can learn to 'celebrate the butterflies' – it will work."

In my fourth book title, I was so direct about my "Just Like" thinking that it actually revealed itself in the very first word of the title – *Like A Pelican In The Desert – Leadership Redefined: Beyond Awkwardness.* I compared "out of place" sensations within leadership that seem awkward to how a pelican (a large water bird) must feel in a desert (a dry, barren spanse of land).

In this very book, my eighth book, I once again use "Just Like" thinking to exhort a reach-for-the-sky attitude – hence, *Think Like A Giraffe.*

I am certainly aware that the preferred term is actually "just as" – not "just like." However, I have never experienced "just as" to be as descriptive, precise, or powerful as "just like." "Just like" seems to emphasize the "comparing" activity or virtue behind this breed of thinking.

The Just Like Principle

If you are interested in a more thorough discussion of "Just Like" thinking, may I suggest *Celebrate The Butterflies – Presenting With Confidence In Public.* Helpful reading can be found in Chapter 7 ("Just As"). For our purposes, "Just Like" thinking is a very creative connection, hinge, extension, elaboration, or hybrid interpretation. It can lead to higher levels of creativity and performance.

Please allow me to share with you a rather exhaustive cataloguing of some "Just Like" examples. I do believe this will prove to be very helpful to you in raising levels of your creativity and your performance. As a matter of fact, within the past few days, I have received several letters from audience participants who wanted to affirm what a fresh application of "Just Like" thinking had meant to their creativity.

Some Just Like Examples:

- Just like someone decided to take free water, bottle it and sell it, why can I not take free air (oxygen), bottle it and sell it? (Incidentally, they are doing that very successfully in Canada.)
- Just like someone long ago decided to sell

beverage at a gas station, why can I not sell hamburgers in a home supply center?
- Just like someone now sells hamburgers in a home supply center, why can I not open a bank in a grocery store?
- Just like someone now offers banking services in a grocery store, why can I not take the pharmacy to the clinic, the clinic to the neighborhood, the pizza to the house, and the world to my personal computer?
- If he can become closer with his team by being open and vulnerable, then why can't I do that – just like he did?
- If a major corporation can take a failure, a huge mistake, and turn it into one of their most profitable products, then maybe I can do that – just like they did.

It is possible that Jack Canfield and Mark Victor Hansen used "Just Like" thinking when they thought that, because people recognized value in chicken soup for the body, then according to the "Just Like" principle, people might value books on *Chicken Soup For The Soul* – and were they ever right! "Just like chicken soup is good for the body, why can it not be good for something else?"

The Just Like Principle

We have known for years that there was value behind team teaching. Now, people are saying: "Just like there is value behind team teaching, why should there not be value behind team learning!"

For decades we have recognized that lines could carry voices (telephone). Years ago, it was "Just Like" thinking that led to: "Just like they send sound over lines, why can we not now send images over lines (fax machine)?"

"Just Like" thinking is very powerful stuff. If you are disciplined in your "Just Like" thinking, it will help you reach for and attain new spheres of creativity and performance. Be determined here – "Just Like" thinking is worth your every effort. Your papers, letters, memos, reports, articles, do not have to be the "same old thing" for those who read them or for you as you write them. Fresh, creative approaches, spawned by your "Just Like" thinking will garner the reader's attention and invigorate you.

Your capacity to recapture focus can be enhanced by "Just Like" thinking. Your ability to move beyond "the as is" to "the will be" can be improved. Your penchant for growth within a culture of change can be propelled "Just Like" thinking merits and mandates your discipline!

THINK LIKE A GIRAFFE

In Summary:

- You will never be your most creative self if you do not seek to understand "Just Like" thinking.
- "Just Like" thinking is "associational" thinking. It is thinking that looks for threads that can be compared.
- You can find examples of "Just Like" thinking, thought-starters, idea- igniters, all around you.
- "Just Like" thinking is worth all the discipline you can muster.

The fundamental activity of Chapter Nine is – *comparing!*

Reminder Formula:
"Just Like" thinking equals
a centerpiece for creativity.

CHAPTER 10

The Back Pocket Principle

The Protecting

My memory about my father is not as keen as it should be. I suspect that has to do with his early death, and perhaps with some things that were going on with me during my teenage years. However, I do remember very strongly his insistence that I never leave the house without money. It was very important to him that I not be compromised into "an off-guard" situation.

THINK LIKE A GIRAFFE

On many occasions I would tell him that I had sufficient money. Quite often he would respond: "Oh I want to be sure you have enough. Here – put this in your back pocket – just in case – for some extra protection."

Now I certainly do not want to write anything that would discourage your excitement about increasing levels of your creativity and performance – that is the very essence of this book. But I do want to remind you, and at the same time remind myself, that sometimes we need to be very sure that we have something "in the back pocket," just in case our big dream does not materialize. Please understand me here. This is not an admonition against adventure, against reaching-for-the-sky. It is simply a caution related to the composite theme that appears throughout this book: "any strength taken too far can become a weakness."

Though I exhort a reach-for-the-sky attitude in creativity and performance, though I understand that one can certainly be too cautious, I had to address the reality that, on occasion, one should indeed be cautious. One can certainly leave what one has too early.

Caution

Let me elaborate. Sometimes, our big dreams can get the best of us. We can become all excited about that which we can create, about the levels at which we can perform in relationship to a new venture, and we prematurely leave what is working for us at this moment.

It is not unusual for an audience participant to come up to me after a presentation and ask: "Mr. Gower, I'd like to become a professional speaker. What do I need to do?" That type of question is asked of me and my colleagues in this wonderful industry time and again. Each of us repeatedly has to wrestle with the way we answer that question. We do not want to dwarf another's excitement about presentations he or she could create, about books he or she could write, about a high level of performance that one could exhibit in a new venture related to professional speaking, consulting, training and writing.

Neither, however, do we want to give the impression that this is an "easy" business – for it certainly is not.

Do Not Throw Common Sense To The Wind

Please hear me correctly here. This does not say "throw caution to the wind" – neither does it say "throw common sense to the wind." Any strength taken too far, that of a rational reserve or that of an aggressive reach-for-the-sky attitude, can become more of a liability than an asset.

Sometimes it makes a tremendous amount of sense to stick with what you have – even as you seek to create something new. This is precisely what I did many years ago. I was the General Manager of a 100,000 watt FM radio station. I did not immediately quit that work and pursue public speaking. With the cooperation of those with whom I worked, I actually eased myself out of one, into the other. For several years, I was actually involved in doing both – participating in a broadcast business, and pursuing my own speaking profession.

This type of scenario will not be possible for everyone. However, many of my colleagues who are now exceptionally successful in their professional speaking businesses began by slowly building their speaking businesses, always knowing that if it did not work out there was something in the "back pocket."

Gradualism Is An Art

The situation for you may not exactly mirror those previously discussed. There will of course be variations. However, especially if you are contemplating a career change, or even if you are seeking to expand your creativity and performance levels, you must seriously seek to balance common sense with raw courage, the given with the possible, the reassuring with the risky, the protecting with the pursuing. The guide toward growth in one's creativity and performance must be centered around this fragile balance.

Please always keep in your back pocket the idea that you do not have to totally leave a position, an idea, a persuasion before you create a new one.

What you keep in your back pocket, the "solid and steady" you currently have, may be something you will not want to totally release until you feel established in a new venture.

"Backing Off" Is Also An Art

Sometimes, the very idea of the "new venture" is not a good idea. Accordingly, when appropriate, we must hold something else in our back pocket – an ability to "let it go." We must back off – completely. A significant think-like-a-giraffe principle is this: "At least occasionally, when it comes to your efforts at creating something new, there is no penalty for early withdrawal to protect what you have." Develop the "back pocket" discipline.

We must balance "sticking to it" and "letting it go." Discipline is still a key here. Determination remains a very important factor! This is serious business!

Do not allow them to stop making back pockets! Back pockets hold precious commodities.

Focus on the arts – gradualism and "backing off."

The Back Pocket Principle

In Summary:

- It takes a keen discipline to remember the back pocket.
- The back pocket may provide you with an opportunity for exploration and a solid base of support at the same time.
- Sometimes, it is best to say "no" or "no, not now" or "yes, but gradually."
- We must be determined to protect our back pockets.
- Focus on the arts – gradualism and "backing off."

The fundamental activity of Chapter Ten is – *protecting!*

Reminder Formula:
Blue jeans minus back pockets
equal discomfort and dysfunction.

CHAPTER 11

The Eliminate– Duplicate Principle
The Eliminating/Duplicating

I have seen it in most every situation imaginable.

A high school wrestler, observing that he has lost his last four matches, views the films of the matches. He notices that, in each instance, right before he was pinned, he wiped sweat from his brow. Once he learned to tolerate the sweat in crucial situations, he would win three matches in a row – each victory resulting from the elimination of the error that he had made before.

THINK LIKE A GIRAFFE

A parent yields to a toddler's pressure too often. The child begins significant growth only when the parent eliminates an incessant acquiescing, and replaces it with a well-defined discipline.

A Chief Executive Officer finds that Senior Vice Presidents are leaving the company at an alarming rate. Retention becomes a reality only when the Chief Executive Officer eliminates his excessively abrasive leadership style, and substitutes with a style that pays more attention to affirmation. Paying attention creates retention.

A college student struggles with an introductory course in Public Speaking. She appears convinced that: (1) she has nothing to say, (2) if she did have something to say, no one would really listen. Once she positively responds to an encouragement to eliminate her negative thinking, she learns to pay the "preparation price," and her nervous energy transcends anxiety and approaches anticipation.

An author submits proposal after proposal to a plethora of literary agents and publishers. He receives nothing but rejection letters. Once he isolates a common factor, a related thread that seems to glue the rejection letters together, and once he modifies content or proposal structure, once he eliminates the

---

The Eliminate/Duplicate Principle

prior error, he receives more than one expression of acceptance of his proposal.

A Human Resource Director notices that the team members are no longer merely working or quitting; many actually appear to quit before they quit. It is only when the Human Resource Director examines his company's "us-them" policy, seeks to eliminate those barriers which separate, and replaces them with bridges which connect, that team members recapture their enthusiasm about their work.

Elimination

What did the high school wrestler, the parent, the Chief Executive Officer, the college student, the author, the Human Resource Director have in common with each other?

Each isolated that which was a source of frustration. Isolation led to elimination. Elimination led to creation – the creativity that birthed a better way – and a better performance.

The high school wrestler isolated and eliminated the move to wipe sweat from his brow, and created a defensive and offensive focus – a focus that was unobtrusive in nature and victorious in results.

THINK LIKE A GIRAFFE

A parent isolated and eliminated a yielding to the toddler's tantrum of temper. He created a discipline that demanded respect and built boundaries – boundaries that ultimately led to the freedom for a child to become a man.

The Chief Executive Officer isolated and eliminated his preoccupation with excessive weakness confrontation and created a specific "win review" policy which ultimately equaled higher levels of performance for individuals, and for the corporation.

The college student isolated and eliminated her negative attitude about speaking in public and created a more positive approach. She began to accept herself. She prepared her presentation in a manner that approached excellence based on both her creativity and her increased performance. The obliteration of personality was no longer the issue – appropriate modification of her behavior led to her hope and to her excitement.

The author isolated and eliminated the flaw in his proposal or in the content of the manuscript. What resulted was the creation of a proposal that mandated a "yes." This proposal eventually equaled many of his books being in print.

The Eliminate/Duplicate Principle

The Human Resource Director isolated and eliminated the walls that separate "us from them." The result was the creation of a policy that exhorted a bonding – a mutually beneficial relationship, not a relationship that was exclusive and self-serving in nature.

In each case, the think-like-a-giraffe principle, the reach-for-the-sky attitude was entrenched in this truth: "sometimes, for creativity and performance to be increased, something must be eliminated."

And, on occasion, something must be duplicated!

Duplication

It is certainly not always isolation and elimination that equal creativity and maximum performance. Quite often, isolation and duplication birth the growth that we so desire.

Today, I learned of Og Mandino's passing. Just a few months ago, I was talking with him about one of his latest books – *The Spellbinder's Gift*. I will never forget some of the last words he shared with me. He indicated that he was going to be writing another book. When I asked him what the subject of that book would be, he responded in words similar to these, "Whatever the good Lord has in mind."

Well, I think it is fair to say that when the good Lord gifted us with Og Mandino, he "had in mind" a man blessed with skills of storytelling, insight, humor and humility.

Og could duplicate the essence of his style in book after book. From *The Greatest Salesman In The World* to *The Christ Commission*, from *The Choice* to *Og Mandino's University Of Success*, from *The Return Of The Ragpicker* to *The Twelfth Angel,* Og isolated, duplicated, enhanced and created masterpiece after masterpiece.

Og certainly is not the only example of duplication that comes to my mind at this writing.

Just this past weekend, Evander Holyfield shocked many, but not all, when he duplicated for the third time, a determination and a style that would gift him with the nomenclature that equals maximum performance – "World Champion!"

How do bestselling authors and world champions continue to perform so well? They create! They isolate, duplicate, and even improve. They isolate "what works." They duplicate it. Then, they sculpt and chisel and enhance!

The Eliminate/Duplicate Principle

How do the same coaches create championship teams after championship teams? They duplicate systems that worked the season before. They duplicate plays that worked the week before. They duplicate procedures that other teams found effective against this week's particular opponent.

How do politicians win elections? They study polls, read surveys, find out what worked before, and duplicate.

How does a golfer improve his score? He finds out what grip, what stance, what club, what club position, what ball led to his best score! He isolates, duplicates and creates better scores.

A pianist duplicates finger movements until they appear as one with piano keys. The process grows and equals maximum performance – that is, until further duplication redefines maximum performance.

Duplication works. It may not always work. And sometimes it may only work when it follows isolation, elimination, and new start after new start.

A leader, without an abundance of degrees, simply catalogues all the mistakes she has observed other leaders make day after day, year after year, decade after decade. She develops a style based on the elimination of that composite of errors she has observed in others. She duplicates this style of effective eliminations, and in cyclical fashion, series after series, albeit it with dips and detours, she redefines her creativity and performance.

Creativity and maximum performance are never static – nor are they event. Creativity and performance equal the process that may be significantly and repeatedly expanded through elimination and or duplication.

Eliminate the flaws. Duplicate the function of positive force. And never, never forget – in the process, there will be detours.

If you are serious about developing your reach-for-the-sky attitude, then pay special attention to the discipline of elimination and duplication. Constantly seek to eliminate flaws. Duplicate and expand functions that yield higher levels of creativity and performance.

Remember, you never really get there. You are always heading there – heading on your determined way!

The Eliminate/Duplicate Principle

In Summary:

- The discipline that is elimination can be very helpful.
- The determination that is duplication can be very helpful.
- Both elimination and duplication must be preceded by isolation.
- Both elimination and duplication can be followed by enhancement.

The fundamental activities of Chapter Eleven are– *eliminating and duplicating!*

Reminder Formula:
Elimination and Duplication
can equal a creative combination.

Part Three
The Delight

Discouragement's friend was fright,
Choking still journey's delight.
Encouragement's mate took the chance,
Gifting her with the will to dance.

DANCE

CHAPTER 12

The Intellectual Workout Principle
The Limbering

The 1996 Olympics in Atlanta gifted the world with a spectacular showcase of form and strength – none of which would have been possible had the participants not taken part in numerous physical workouts.

If physical workouts benefit athletes, if physical workouts lay the foundation for victory, then mental workouts and intellectual dancing pay huge dividends for the one reaching for greater levels of creativity and higher peaks of performance.

THINK LIKE A GIRAFFE

For our purposes, the "intellectual workout" equals a plethora of "limbering - up" exercises. It is the limbering that will prepare us for giraffle-like-thinking.

We must choose this limbering. We must choose to be pliable, flexible – we must bend in the positive sense of the word.

As you dance toward greater creativity, and as you delight in higher levels of performance, you will become more and more convinced that your success had a great deal to do with your limbering exercises that preceded the crucial series of events.

To participate in the dance that equals limbering is to:

1. Surround yourself with those whose thought-life factor you appreciate.
2. Read to your children (you may be surprised at what a limbering effect this will have on you – as well as on them).
3. Travel every state in our nation. This can stimulate you.
4. Pursue meaningful television – stop belittling all television as violent, obscene, or a waste of time.
5. Play with the children – become amazed at how wise your children are.

The Intellectual Workout Principle

6. Participate in the limbering exercises that are centered around speed-reading – compete against yourself and compare your retention scores day after day or week after week.
7. Particularly seek to enjoy the game shows on television that require an intellectual stretching on your part.
8. Attend as many academic bowls as you can.
9. Write a one hundred word philosophy of life from your point of view – then condense it down to fifty words – then to twenty-five – then to five.
10. Limber up by finding true wisdom through Him.
11. Allow your "mental endorphins" to help you do your Creativity Dance.

It is important to state here that your pursuit toward higher levels of creativity and performance does not have to be something to be endured. It can be something to be experienced in a positive way – something to be enjoyed. Limbering does not have to be interpreted as that which exclusively prepares one for dancing. Limbering can be considered as dancing. I fundamentally believe that if you seek to enjoy your limbering, even if it is a struggle for you (like that discussed in the following chapter), you will be more effective in your quest for higher levels of creativity and greater performance-peaks.

Delight is a choice and "limbering up" helps make the choice easier.

In Summary:

- Intellectual, or limbering, workouts are just as important as physical workouts.
- The dancing that equals a mental-limbering is crucial to creativity.
- Delight is a choice.
- The dance that equals limbering can help you enjoy the journey toward your sky-destination.

The fundamental activity of Chapter Twelve is – *limbering.*

Reminder Formula:
Dancing before and during the dreaming may equal dancing after the dreaming!

CHAPTER 13

The Struggle Principle

The Struggling

O ur conversation occurred at the Brookwood Train Station in Atlanta. I was headed home, he for New York. Soon we were discussing our vocations.

I would learn that he was a choreographer. I had never before conversed with a choreographer of his stature. So I was determined to garner as much knowledge as I could from him. I indicated I would soon be writing a book on creativity and maximum performance and told him I would appreciate his input. He willingly responded to my question: "What fuels your creativity?"

He had already shared several answers, most of which have been covered elsewhere in this book, when he mentioned one answer that directly relates to the subject of this chapter, and interestingly enough, to the issue of choreography and dancing.

He shared, "I have also found that struggle can breed my creativity." I should not have been as shocked as I must have appeared, because on further reflection, I resurrected several situations where tension had ultimately gifted me with an unexpected inventory of fresh approaches.

Miscues and the tension which precede or follow them can lead to additional or "double-fault" mistakes, or they can serve as a crucible for breeding much more effective responses and results – a new "reach-for-the-sky" attitude that can equal a bounty of performance-fruits. Just as there is a dance that equals "limbering," there is also a dance called "struggling."

My rumination about my own struggles, and my research into the creativity that has emanated from the tension of many others, lead me to share some common threads which may help you rediscover the potential that can travel within tension.

The Struggle Principle

Remember, we are at this very point in the third section of our book – the Delight section. The very fact that the choreographer identified creativity with struggling, seems to suggest that the delight that is related to creativity is not isolated to a final moment – completion, destination – or even to pleasantries and ease. The delight that is related to creativity can also occur during the journey – even if the journey involves struggle. Now, let me share three common threads which can evolve out of the struggle-dance:

- Tension can cause avoidance.
- Tension can cause adjustment.
- Tension can cause acceleration.

Avoidance

Struggle can mandate avoidance – "I will not pursue this anymore. It is counterproductive. By avoiding this, I will be free to focus more effectively and perform more efficiently."

It is possible for tension to reveal the value behind positive avoidance, the wisdom that can travel with "early withdrawal." Sometimes, the most creative thing one can do is to quit spinning wheels that go nowhere or even cease spinning wheels that only appear to go in a backwards direction. As we have discussed in earlier chapters, the situation may have immense tutorial value if the individual learns from the excessive tension, and allows that tension to lead to the positive avoidance of similar abuse-efforts in the future.

Sometimes, reaching for the sky may mandate a halting, a stopping, an avoidance which simply and profitably leads the giraffe to another tree – even to another sky-place. A reach-for-the-sky attitude in creativity and maximum performance may call for avoidance. Tension may help you hear the call.

What Does The Avoidance That Tension Can Cause Look Like?

The avoidance that we are discussing here could lead to: 1) change in vocation, 2) geographical change, 3) a total turn-about within the heart. Before I close out this section, let me share one observation as to items one and two, another observation about item three.

Before your perceived tension leads you to change vocation or geography, be very sure you are not seeking to inappropriately solve an internal struggle with an external remedy. Read *When Your Work Matters To God,* by Sherman and Hendricks, for additional information about this particular issue. I think you will find that book also helpful as you seek to ferret out for yourself whether or not a turn-about is called for within your heart .

I must be delicate here, but I do want to indicate that I am finding time and again that this heart-issue, even as it relates to creativity and maximum performance, is a spiritual issue. And, for me, God reveals Himself and His Spirit through the Holy Spirit and through His Son, Jesus Christ. It is quite possible that ultimately your tension or struggle will lead you to avoid something or maybe even someone. It may also lead you to Someone. It is also possible that you will ultimately feel like dancing as a result of your experience with struggle.

Adjustment

Tension may not mandate total attitudinal and behavioral retreat. Tension may not only benefit your creativity and performance by leading you away from counterproductive, and even regressive activity, it can also gift you by revealing a rough spot that is in need of some alignment, or adjustment.

Tension can call for total abstinence or avoidance, or it can simply ask for evaluation of a particular hurdle. The giraffe may find one tree's leaves totally inapproachable. He may find another tree loaded with leaves, unusually high up in the tree. If the giraffe is to reach the leaves of this second tree, he may need to adjust his approach, his stance – even move and stick out his neck.

What Do The Adjustments That Tension Can Precipitate Look Like?

The tension or struggle which elicits adjustment may call for: refinement in study, diminishment in intensity, alignment in relationships.

Refinement In Study

Tension resulting from abuse and misuse of a particular frustration must be addressed here. I hope this personal illustration will prove helpful.

The Struggle Principle

Early in my professional speaking career, I became frustrated with the way I was using huge chunks of time on airplanes. I enjoyed the flying, and still do, I just became increasingly frustrated with the way I was managing hours and days spent on planes.

I could have chosen to avoid flying. That would have been foolish. I could have chosen to change the airline company with which I had flown for so many years. That would have been futile. Instead, I finally chose to evaluate the stewardship of my time. That was fruitful. It was an especially creative thing to do.

In 1990, I decided that I had taken enough naps, read enough magazines, talked enough with fellow passengers, watched enough movies and listened to enough classical music.

Oh, I would of course make some exceptions, but the frustration and tension that accompanied my perceived misuse of significant amounts of my time resulted in a major adjustment in my relationship to time. I would begin to use my time much more wisely.

I realigned my study habits, and wrote seven books over a five-year period. Most of the writing occurred on airplanes.

This was not merely a reach-for-the-sky

approach – it was a reach-in-the-sky attitude. This was an adjustment caused by tension which led to creativity.

Diminishment In Intensity

There is another alignment which must be addressed here. Diminishment in the intensity with which you work and perform may be the alignment that is mandated here. You say, "Whoa – the adjustment that tension elicits should equal an increase, not a decrease, in the level of the intensity of effort." And, we will address that point shortly, because in many situations, tension will force more, not less, intensity.

However, this should not be the case in every scenario. There will be times when the adjustment which tension calls for will be "slow down," not "speed up." The adjustments that flow from the tension of excessive intensity which can deter creativity and diminish performance may look like: more attention to journey, less preoccupation with destination, less internal scrutiny, less comparison with others, a visit to the catalogue in your mind that holds memories of insights shared with you by your favorite teacher or perhaps even a grandparent, and more time alone.

Alignment In Relationships

I wanted the previous section to conclude with "More Time Alone" because I thought it would serve as a helpful segue into the "Alignment In Relationships" portion of this chapter.

The tension which can produce positive creativity and performance-results may have earlier led a person to examine that tension. He may later decide to adjust, and eventually he may make significant alignments in relationships.

The manner in which you relate with other people affects them and it affects you!

You will not be able to align them. Neither will you be able to align for them. But you *can* be responsible for your efforts in aligning your relationships.

You can move closer to excitement and away from exasperation – closer to stability, and away from irritability. Your "at-easeness" in your relationships, developed through the alignment-adjustment process, will free you for think-like-a-giraffe creativity and an attained reach-for-the-sky performance.

Specific relationship alignment responses include: finding rest in Him, fueling encouragement cycles for others, and favoring win reviews over lost reviews.

Finding Rest in Him

Please emphasize to yourself, time and again, the primary function of this relationship with Him as a foundation for the alignment of all other relationships.

Centuries ago, a feisty St. Augustine would repeatedly respond to his mother's wake-up calls with "Anon, Anon" (not now, not now). Later, he appeared to find himself uttering that same expression to his Heavenly Father. Significant tension developed within him. For St. Augustine, the tension led to an adjustment. It led to an alignment. It led him to say, "I find no rest, until I rest in Thee."

And, so it is with us!

Fueling Encouragement Cycles For Others

You're either doing one or the other. You are encouraging or discouraging them. Why waste time discouraging them when that discouragement could harm both you and them? Why waste time discouraging them when in reality your discouraging them actually, and emphatically, boomerangs back into you, stifling your creativity and limiting your performance?

Do you want to be more creative? Do you want to raise the levels of your performance? Then, encourage others. The more time you spend encouraging others, and the less time you give to discouraging others, the more you will celebrate that which is mutually beneficial. The encouragement-dance is helpful for them – and for you.

Favoring Win Reviews Over Loss Reviews

Adjustment in relationship-alignments will always be called for when you incessantly succeed in expressing loss reviews (confrontations) with others, more than you succeed in expressing win reviews (affirmations) with others.

It is my experience that excessive and specific, loss reviews, at the point of another's need for improvement or weakness, will actually subtract from your creativity and performance levels.

However, your genuine and specific, win reviews at the point of another's strengths can actually add to, if not multiply, your own creativity and performance totals. Giraffes do not subtract. They multiply.

Acceleration

Thinking like a giraffe does not happen by chance! On occasion, thinking like a giraffe occurs because Tension caught your focus in a positive way, and caused you to choose change – not chance or luck. Normally, it is not luck or chance that speeds you up and hastens your pace.

No, many of us grow because we heard Tension beckoning us to change – to begin a new dance! We had been traveling below minimum speed, nowhere near the speed limit. We certainly were not dancing. Why, we were barely shuffling our feet. Finally, Tension was fed up with us, and had something to say. Tension said: "Get up, go to it, speed up, accelerate, dance!"

Specifically, the adjustment of acceleration includes: dreaming harder, digging deeper, dancing faster.

Dreaming Harder

Press your dream pedal more firmly. Study your "dream-a-meter." Is it where it was last month, or last year, or last decade? Is the sky you're reaching for still too low? Reach for fulfillment, dance toward purpose and place, dance for meaning. Accelerate your mind-vision! Increase your dream-speed!

Digging Deeper

Tension, fear, or frustration may mandate the acceleration of your dreaming. It may also suggest that you put your digging effort into overdrive.

It is simple; sometimes we have to go to work – really go to work! Sometimes, we must work smarter, study with a redefined intensity, even play with a magnified vigor.

Dancing Faster

Our magnificent play-vigor merits special attention. If your tension eventually beckons you toward an examination and escalation of your play, your dancing, your delighting, then it may have served you very well.

Believe me, there is a direct correlation between your creativity and your performance levels – and the frequency and intensity with which you play. Sometimes, rocking and rolling is not only good – it is great!

Of course, this is another illustration of a strength taken too far becoming a growth point. If one plays all the time, one becomes terribly frustrated. But, in appropriate doses, play need not be a novacaine which numbs creativity and performance. Appropriate play, appropriate dancing and delighting, may serve as stimulants for creativity and performance.

The Tension Of Paranoia

Before I close this chapter on tension and its relationship to the struggle-dances called Avoidance, Adjustment, and Acceleration, let me lift up a tremendous and innovative discussion of the positive fruits that can flow from tension. The discussion I lift up can be found in Andrew S. Grove's *Only The Paranoid Survive.*

As President and Chief Executive Officer of Intel Corporation, Mr. Grove can personally testify to the value of constructive paranoia within a tension-filled world.

The Struggle Principle

His subtitle, *How To Exploit The Crisis Points That Challenge Every Company And Career,* is in itself a reminder that frustration can give birth to creativity. You will find this excellent book listed in the Recommended Reading section beginning on page 177. It certainly merits your serious consideration. In my opinion, Andrew S. Grove is a superb dancer – creator – performer!

The struggle-dance that travels along with our efforts at raising creativity and performance, may equal three different dances: the Avoidance, the Adjustment or the Acceleration. If the appropriate dance leads toward higher levels of creativity and performance, it may well have been a dance worth dancing!

In Summary:

- There are three main struggle-dances for your consideration: the Avoidance, the Adjustment, the Acceleration.
- Tension can be a great tutor.
- Struggle may eventually prove to be your friend.
- Often, Delight is initially camouflaged as something else!

THINK LIKE A GIRAFFE

The fundamental activity of Chapter Thirteen in our guide is – *struggling!*

Reminder Formula:
Avoidance plus Adjustment plus Acceleration can equal the Dance called Optimum Achievement.

CHAPTER 14

The S-O-O-S Principle

The Driving

If "SOS" is the military's method for calling for external help, then "S-O-O-S" is your method for calling for your best self – for internal help.

Ultimately, the dance which is associated with the journey and destination related to creativity and performance is a dance you must dance. Though a plethora of external resources is available, the key call you must make is the call within – the "S-O-O-S."

For the purposes of this book, our "S-O-O-S" Principle equals:
- Start your own engine.
- Open up the throttle.
- Observe the caution flags.
- Stay the course.

Start Your Own Engine

To think like a giraffe is to take responsibility for your own creativity and your own performance. To possess a reach-for-the-sky attitude is to dance your own dance. Your creativity and performance levels will not rise because you are sitting around and waiting for others to pull the choke, start the engine, do the work. If you want to drive, start your own engine! Across the country, leaders tell me that what they appreciate the most within their team members is their capacity to self-start. Ultimately, there is really no other effective way to start – than to self-start your own engine.

Open Up The Throttle

When appropriate, be willing to run full speed. When appropriate, be willing to take the risks which separate the leaves high up in the tree from those so close to the ground. When appropriate, dance without allowing the routine and the ordinary to intimidate you. If you want to drive, open up the throttle – when appropriate. But again, do not throw common sense and caution to the wind.

Observe The Caution Flags

Did you notice how many times I referred to the phrase "when appropriate" in the prior section? Well, I did that for a reason. Many people feel that risk always travels with raising one's creativity and performance levels. Well, that is certainly true on occasion. But, it is certainly not always true!

You can be creative and cautious at the same time. For example, you must be very cautious if the welfare of someone else is at hand; you must also be very cautious if your welfare is at hand.

If you have ever observed a giraffe on the lookout for lions, or even in a splayed position seeking to protect a smaller giraffe, you will certainly reach the conclusion that giraffes have not thrown caution to the wind, and neither should we. We should observe caution flags – particularly when they warn of possible harm for us or someone else. If you want to drive up your creativity and performance levels, observe the caution flags!

Stay The Course

It may well be that the most important ingredient in growing, both when it comes to creativity and performance, is the ingredient of commitment, determination, discipline – dancing on the track with a respect for staying and finishing the course. Dance until song's end!

This is a very brief chapter. But hopefully, every time you hear about automobile racing, you will think of this "Just Like" example – *when you want to think like a giraffe: start your own engine, open up the throttle, observe the caution flags, and stay the course.*

The S-O-O-S Principle

In Summary:

- You must be responsible for starting your own engine.
- You must be determined to open up your throttle.
- You must not throw caution and common sense to the wind.
- You must stay on the course.
- If you want to win your race, you must stay on the track – driving and dancing until song's end.

The fundamental activity of Chapter Fourteen is – *driving!*

Reminder Point:
The driver in the race equals you.

CHAPTER 15

The Clogging Principle

The Clogging

Perched between Clayton and Dillard, Georgia, is a hamlet that served as "clogging central" for me and my high school classmates. Slabs of hardwood became dance floor for me and my friends in a place they still call Mountain City.

The clog is a hybrid dance – almost a marriage between square dancing and line dancing. It is not easy. You are either very good at it – or you are awful. On Saturday nights, "Awful" became my middle name.

Nevertheless, as I have been thinking about a

creative manner in which to begin wrapping up our time together, the acronym of C-L-O-G-G-I-N-G has continued to surface within my head. If the literal "clogging" includes a fundamental maneuver – a subtle, yet vigorous kick-shuffle, a raising of the heel so it makes contact with hard wood in such a way as to make a mountain of noise, then our C-L-O-G-G-I-N-G can equal first steps toward a fundamental review.

When it comes to developing your skills at creativity and performance, you can pursue C-L-O-G-G-I-N-G:

- *Caress* yourself – you will never be at your best as long as you constantly chastise yourself.
- *Laugh* at yourself – if you want to make significant contributions with your life, do not always take yourself too seriously.
- *Obligate* some of yourself to volunteer work – I cannot overemphasize how invigorating and stimulating volunteer work can be.
- *Greet* each day as a gift – the preciousness of life comes twenty-four hours at a time.
- *Gather* around yourself a group of positive cloggers – enjoy each other.
- *Inoculate* yourself against excessive preoccupation with others' expectations of

you, and against totally unreasonable expectations that you have of yourself. The disease of "expectations run wild" can frustrate the most determined giraffes.

- *Navigate* yourself through The Wastelands into your Gain Forest – the navigation can equal maturation.
- *Gift* yourself with a mountain of benefits – your own M-O-U-N-T-A-I-N C-I-T-Y:

- *Motivate* yourself – no one else can.
- *Observe* "quiet time" as a calm before your dance.
- *Understand* yourself as "just one!" – not "just one?"
- *Notice* that sometimes to think like a giraffe is to optimize, oscillate, observe and obligate like a goose.
- *Try* to incorporate "just-like" thinking into your search for further development in your creativity and performance.
- *Appreciate* The Gain Forest as that grand reservoir of creativity and performance resources that transcends The Wastelands.

THINK LIKE A GIRAFFE

- *Imagine* yourself thinking like a giraffe –
  reaching for the sky, sticking your neck
  out, achieving your goals.
- *Never* perceive creativity and performance
  as event – they are process.
- *Comprehend* the marvelous mix between
  From Within and From Without as that
  which can equal Fulfillment Within.
- *Instill* within yourself an appreciation for
  the "I's": Inspiration, Interpolation,
  Introspection, Imagination, and *Isolate*
  your Frustration and Accomplishment
  Precipitators.
- *Trust* the tutorial value of tension in
  Avoidance , Adjustment, and Acceleration.
- *Yield* to the One who created you – to the
  One who gifted you with creativity and
  performance.

The literal Mountain City is a delightful city.
You will also find that this "Mountain City" will gift
you with delight.

The Clogging Principle

In Summary:

- Do your own C-L-O-G-G-I-N-G.
- Take responsibility for your own
  M-O-U-N-T-A-I-N C-I-T-Y.

The fundamental activity of Chapter Fifteen
is – *clogging!*

Reminder Formula:
C-L-O-G-G-I-N-G can equal your growth!

CHAPTER 16

The Nothing But Net Principle

The Being Human

Is The Net The Ally Or The Villain?

I coached basketball. I was a very good basketball coach. I tried to play basketball. I was awful.

There was a phrase that they never uttered to describe my shots. However, this phrase was used to describe the basketball shots of my players time and time again. When the ball would go where it was to go, when the ball would not touch backboard or iron at all, the appropriate phrase describing the masterful shot would be, "nothing but net!"

Well, as we begin to close our time together, let me remind you that the world of technocracy is running toward us head-on. We can allow technocracy to be our ally, or we can allow technocracy – the Internet and all that travels with it, to paralyze us, to literally sap away our creative and performance juices.

Certainly technocracy can gift us. We see its marvelous benefits daily. In health care alone, technocracy has saved millions of lives. But, taken too far – taken to the point of "nothing but net" – we could find ourselves little more than robots. Our creativity and performance will move closer and closer to the ground.

"Idea Lessness" And "Idea-Evaporation"

We know that we are susceptible to diseases called "idea lessness" and "idea-evaporation." We know that "idea lessness" is caused by the blurring, the boring, or the burning. Its roots equal lack of clarity, lack of enthusiasm, and lack of energy.

We know that "idea-evaporation," is caused by both internal and external catalysts. In many instances, we have the information – we just do not

use it.   Here, information minus implementation
equals idea-evaporation. In other instances, we human
beings rely on technocracy too much – so much that
we allow our minds, our creative juices, to atrophy.

Idea-Discovery And Idea-Retention

What else do we understand about ourselves?
We understand that we must keep ourselves fit for
both "idea-retention" and "idea-discovery." We must
not become utterly, totally, dependent upon computers and the like.

Again, technocracy has gifted us in a thou-
sand ways. Technocracy is not our threat. Our depen-
dence upon technocracy is the threat. "The Net" can
help you discover and retain ideas. Depend too much
on "The Net" – you may stumble badly.   When
appropriate, "The Net" can help you create more and
more, and perform effectively – and even more
effectively still. Abuse it, however, and "The Net"
will stifle your creativity and dwarf your performance.

"The Net" can help you deal with three major
causes of "idea-loss": fatigue, frustration and focus-
void. "The Net" can also help you pursue the "three

THINK LIKE A GIRAFFE

R's" of "idea-discovery": recognition of a void, research for an answer, and response – both attitudinally and behaviorally. There is tremendous value in "The Net."

Nevertheless, may I caution you – *Never forget, there is more to you than all of the computers in the world.* In the case of human resource development, "The Net" can be taken too far. You are not "The Net." You are much more than "The Net." You are human resource! "The Net" need not be your only dancing partner.

For more than a quarter of a century now, I have been observing and studying the development of corporations, associations, and organizations. I have seen how each has been gifted by "The Net." But I do have a very serious concern. My concern is that we may just forget the precious value of human resources.

If we ever allow the workplace to become a "Nothing But Net" place, if we ever forget the marvelous "unity in diversity" that humankind can equal, we will falter. If we ever stop, one by one, thinking-like-a-giraffe and reaching-for-the-sky, then we will tragically experience a massive creativity-evaporation and a catastrophic performance-vacuum!

The Nothing But Net Principle

Your great ideas, your potential for creativity, and your capacity for maximum performance are awful things to ignore! And I must add – please never forget that He made you in His image. Handle with care!

In Summary:

- If "nothing but net" is an accolade in basketball, it can be an asset or an albatross in the human experience.
- Technocracy offers many marvelous gifts to our world.
- Taken too far, these gifts can thwart the human spirit.

The fundamental activity of Chapter Sixteen in our guide is – *being human!*

Reminder Formula:
You equal more than a computer.

CHAPTER 17

The Commencement Principle

The Commencing

Several years ago, my first cousin announced to my grandmother that she was having another child. Now, my grandmother, and each of us, deeply loved this young lady and recognized that she was one of the most gifted mothers we had ever known. But, she had already had several children – perhaps more than my grandmother thought she needed to be responsible for – "way up there, in the cold of Wisconsin."

THINK LIKE A GIRAFFE

So, when my cousin asked Weezie, my one-hundred-year-old grandmother, what name she would suggest for her soon-to-be-born child, my grandmother replied – "Omega!" Now, quite honestly, I do not remember whether that particular child was my cousin's last child or not. But, I am sure that my delightful first cousin continues to focus on the "Alpha" experiences of life much more than she does the "Omega" experiences of life.

And, that is precisely what I invite you to do. This book's end is commencement – and, commencement is an enigma. Commencement is both ending and beginning. It is achievement and anticipation. Commencement is the marriage of Something to Something More. It is a marvelous blending between the finished and the yet-to-be. Commencement is the giraffe who finds leaves high in the tree only to look for those higher still. *Commencement is that perpetual redefining of the sky way up there.*

The bell that commencement rings is not only a "well done" – it is an incessant invitation to grow, to create, to perform, without being totally numbed by "The Net" below, above, and beside. It is an invitation to grow without being paralyzed within a culture of change. It is a mandate to choose

The Commencement Principle

a positive direction, a fierce discipline and a delightful dance. Commencement offers you the privilege to be human.

Being human is a choice. Delight is a choice. Commencement is a choice – and, Commencement is a dance.

It is commencement time. Enjoy the dance!

The fundamental activity of Chapter Seventeen is – *commencing!*

Reminder Formula:
Commencement equals an enigma –
the finished plus the not-yet-done,
the accomplishment plus the anticipation.

CHAPTER 18

Think Like
A Giraffe
The Poem

I f I were to think like a giraffe,
Would it work on my behalf?
He stands tall and reaches for the sky,
I sit and cry "my oh my."

He takes his neck and sticks it out,
I choose to sit and pout and pout.
I say, "It can't get any worse than this."
He says, "Let's give it a different twist."

THINK LIKE A GIRAFFE

"You say things are bad, oh so bad,
And that's why you are always so sad.
Let's see if we can't turn things around.
Quit looking at those leaves so close to the ground.

"Look way up there, high in the tree.
See those leaves—they number three.
They will prove worth your dare,
They'll even help you grow beyond compare.

"Now I'll give you their names,
I will even help you start the games.
But if you want to think like me,
Then you must remember you're the key.

"Leaf number one is the one called Glance,
Beside her, that's her friend Trance.
And leaf number three is the one we call Dance.
Learn these three—they'll give you a new chance.

"Yes, they'll help you walk a new path,
Perhaps even cut your work in half.
Oh my friend, it will work on your behalf,
When you learn to Think Like A Giraffe."

Winter of 1997 – Stephen M. Gower

Recommended Reading

Afterburn, Stephen. Winning At Work Without Losing At Love. Nashville: Thomas Nelson Publishers, 1994.

Alessandra, Tony and Michael J. O'Connor. The Platinum Rule. New York: Warner, 1996.

Block, Peter. Stewardship. San Francisco: Berrett-Koehler Publishers, 1993.

Cameron, Julia. The Vein Of Gold – A Journey To Your Creative Heart. New York: Putnam, 1996.

Canfield, Jack and Mark Victor Hansen, Maida Rogerson, Martin Rutte, and Tim Clauss. Chicken Soup for the Soul at Work – 101 Stories of Courage, Compassion and Creativity in the Workplace. Deerfield Beach, Health Communications, Inc., 1996.

Cathy, S. Truett. It's Easier To Succeed Than To Fail. Nashville: Oliver Nelson, 1989.

Covey, Stephen. The Seven Habits Of Highly Effective People. New York: Simon and Schuster, 1989.

THINK LIKE A GIRAFFE

Gower, Stephen M. <u>Like A Pelican In The Desert - Leadership Redefined: Beyond Awkwardness</u>. Toccoa: Lectern Publishing, 1994.

Gower, Stephen M. <u>The Focus Crisis – Nurturing Focus Within A Culture Of Change</u>. Toccoa: Lectern Publishing, 1996.

Grove, Andrew S. <u>Only The Paranoid Survive</u>. New York: Doubleday, 1996.

Hanson, Peter G. <u>The Joy Of Stress</u>. Kansas City: Andrews and McMeel, 1988.

Harrell, Keith D. <u>Attitude Is Everything</u>. Dubuque: Kendall/Hunt, 1995.

Horn, Sam. <u>Concentration! How To Focus For Success</u>. Menlo Park: Crisp Publications, 1991.

Johnson, Spencer. <u>The Precious Present</u>. New York: Doubleday and Company, 1984.

MacDonald, Gordon. <u>Ordering Your Private Life</u>. Nashville: Oliver Nelson, 1985.

Recommended Reading

Mandino, Og. <u>Mission: Success</u>. New York: Bantam, 1986.

Mandino, Og. <u>Secrets For Success And Happiness</u>. New York: Ballantine, 1995.

McCormack, Mark H. <u>What They Don't Teach You At Harvard Business School</u>. New York: Bantam Books, 1984.

Redfield, James. <u>The Celestine Prophecy</u>. New York: Warner Books, Inc., 1993.

Riley, Pat. <u>The Winner Within</u>. New York: Berkley Books, 1993.

Rohn, Jim. <u>The Seasons Of Life</u>. Irving: Jim Rohn International, 1996.

Rohn, Jim. <u>The Treasury Of Quotes</u>. Irving: Jim Rohn International, 1996.

Sherman, Doug and William Hendricks. <u>Your Work Matters To God</u>. Colorado Springs: NAVPRESS, 1988.

THINK LIKE A GIRAFFE

Von Oech, Roger. <u>A Kick In The Seat Of The Pants</u>. New York: Harper and Row Publishers, 1986.

Von Oech, Roger, Ph.D. <u>A Whack On The Side Of The Head</u>. New York: Warner Books, 1983.

Whyte, David. <u>The Heart Aroused – Poetry And The Preservation Of The Soul In Corporate America</u>. New York: Doubleday, 1996.

Ziglar, Zig. <u>Over The Top</u>. Nashville: Thomas Nelson Publishers, 1994.

About The Author

Stephen M. Gower, CSP, is considered one of the country's most powerful speakers and is a Certified Speaking Professional. This is the highest earned designation of professional achievement presented by the National Speakers Association. Less than 400 professional speakers have earned their CSP worldwide.

Mr. Gower holds a bachelor's degree from Mercer University and a master's degree from Emory University. He is in demand as keynote speaker for international and national conferences and has flown the equivalent of more than 40 times around the globe within the past five years. Stephen has written eight books, and he has produced seven audio tape albums.

As human resource development specialist, he has invested more than 30,000 hours in the past twenty-five years studying issues related to maximum performance. Stephen's philosophy on performance and perception has led many of the world's largest corporations and associations to utilize, and to benefit from, his speaking and consulting services.

For information on Keynote Speeches, Special Occasion Speeches, Seminars, Consulting, Books, and Tapes by Stephen M. Gower, CSP, and for other Gower Growth Systems Products and Services contact:

The Gower Group, Inc.
P. O. Box 714, Toccoa, GA 30577
1-800-242-7404   Fax: 706-886-0465
E-Mail: gowergrp@cyberhighway.net
Visit Our Web Site:
http://www. georgiamagazine.com/gowergrp/